JAILHOUSE RICK

A YOUNG MAN'S TALE FROM
STATE COLLEGE TO
STATE PRISON TO
STATE-OF-THE-ART
TELEVISION COMEDY

RICK BEREN

Copyright © 2024
Cover design: Karen Richardson / Indie Pub Solutions

ISBN: 979-8-218-28631-6

Library of Congress Control Number: 2023920909

Publisher's Cataloging-in-Publication (Provided by Cassidy Cataloguing Services, Inc.)
Names: Beren, Rick, author.
Title: Jailhouse Rick : a young man's tale from state college to state prison to state-of-the art television comedy / Rick Beren.
Description: [Los Angeles, California] : [Berenmind Books], [2024]
Identifiers: ISBN: 979-8-218-28631-6 (paperback) | LCCN: 2023920909
Subjects: LCSH: Beren, Rick. | Television producers and directors--United States--Biography. | Criminals--United States--Biography. | College students--United States--Biography. | Cheers (Television program) | Hollywood (Los Angeles, Calif.) | Self-actualization (Psychology) | LCGFT: Autobiographies. | BISAC: BIOGRAPHY & AUTOBIOGRAPHY / Memoirs. | BIOGRAPHY & AUTOBIOGRAPHY / Criminals & Outlaws. | BIOGRAPHY & AUTOBIOGRAPHY / Entertainment & Performing Arts.
Classification: LCC: PN1992.4.B47 A3 2024 | DDC: 791.450233092--dc23

For my dad, my daughters, and my dogs.
Not in that particular order.

And for my wife Carole, without whom none
of this would be possible, or at least as good.
She took a felon and made him a feline—a little tabby.

Chapter 1: Helter Skelter

As my shoulder gently brushed the smooth, industrial-green cement wall, I turned to look out through the heavily barred windows. Far away, I could see the lazy, rolling brown hills, reminding me of the ones I'd traversed back in Oakland some ten years earlier. I thought of the year 1964. I'd been eight then, and the Beatles had been making their premiere on Ed Sullivan. It's the first time I remember my family sitting around doing something together—and the last.

When I'd come home for dinner back then, it usually sucked. My brother was four years older and a bully, so my life was spent outside until I had to come home. Luckily, there were lots of kids my age in our neighborhood. Our baseball mitts hung from the banana bars as we rode our Schwinn Sting-Ray bikes ($53) with the metallic paint jobs (mine was blue) and the slick tires on their back wheels. We clipped baseball cards (probably worth thousands of dollars now) to the frames with wooden clothespins so the spokes would make fast ticking sounds, *tat tat tat tat tat* like we were racing motorcycles up and down endless dirt lots and the makeshift ramps that we built. We practiced doing wheelies up and down the safe streets. The only danger might have been the distracted housewife barreling past us in her two-ton fake-wood sidings station wagon.

We also rode those bikes miles from our houses and back without anyone knowing (or seemingly giving much of a shit) where the fuck we were.

We hung out for hours in our various above and underground forts, built from wood we appropriated from the newly built houses that were encroaching on our sacred neighborhood. We nabbed packs of cigarettes (Mom's Parliaments with the recessed filters for me) and smoked ourselves sick at age twelve. Later, we stole bottles of our parents' liquor; we'd pour their contents into one container, hold our noses, and then guzzle the mixture of scotch, bourbon, and vodka. It was not one of the best ideas we ever had—not even close.

In the present, my focus returned to the frosted windows, thin, cobwebbed metal wire interlacing each panel. It was difficult to see through them, so I trudged along, shoulders slumped, eyes returned securely to the waxed, buffed linoleum floor. It was so shiny that I could almost discern the reflection of troubled features. That was my face.

I sensed something was awry in the long, wide hallway, so I tentatively peeked back up. The normally bustling area had become uncharacteristically empty. The exit doors, I saw, had been electronically shut and locked. A game of musical chairs had been played, and now I was the only one left in the middle of this suddenly vast space—fifty feet from the nearest doorway, which was securely sealed anyway. From two hundred feet away came the scream: "*Halt!*"

Since I was the only thing left breathing out there, I quickly ascertained the voice was addressing me. By this time, I had become accustomed to complying with any shouted orders, no matter whom they were meant for. Now, a hundred feet away and closing was a heavily armed tactical force. A dozen or so men were approaching, clad with riot helmets and bearing shotguns. I stopped dead in my tracks as they methodically marched toward me.

There was a lone soul in the middle. This person's wrists had been tightly shackled with metal chains at his belt; his bare feet were also bound together at the ankles, so he could only take shuffling six-inch steps. The captive was small, and the escorts around him—each at least a foot taller, with a hundred pounds on him—made him seem even more diminutive. We were all on a collision course, and as far as I could tell, they had no plans to alter their path.

"Up against the wall, motherfucker."

I surmised that, as the only other motherfucker not wearing a guard uniform or armed with deadly weaponry, this meant me. I leaped to obey.

They were within twenty feet. There was nothing now that separated my ass and that concrete wall. They had my full attention. The two behemoths leading the pack leveled their shotguns at me a mere three feet from my head—other than my testicles racing to my throat, I did not move a muscle.

For several moments, I stood there frozen like a palace guard at Windsor Castle—until, glimpsing the piercing look from the slight, menacing figure, my eyes practically popped out of my head. He shot a sideways glance at me, and, through the unkempt hair toppling over much of his face, I met his stare. I shuddered internally. Those eyes were black. Lifeless. His swastika tattoo was visible between them. Prison lore held that if you looked at this guy, you would become hypnotized. I did not want to become a disciple. It was only a couple of years earlier, this person had terrorized an entire nation, especially California.

He made a feint at me. I almost fainted. The twelve huge guards were just barely enough protection . . . for me.

Evil emanated from every pore of the prisoner's body. Charles Manson just smirked.

The party moved on, no one bothering to say when I could move. Blood had not yet returned to all parts of my body, so I wouldn't have been able to anyway. Fear gripped the entire space he invaded. Today it was mine. I choked as a horrible stench still lingered in the forty-foot-wide hall. Either I had shit in my pants, or that dude stank. I stood alone there and wondered, *Did that just happen?*

Here's my story of how a nice little Jewish kid from the very liberal Bay Area, blessed with every form of white privilege, ended up witnessing fellow inmate Charlie Manson as he strolled past me in Vacaville State Prison.

Chapter 2: September

Fresh start! A spanking new semester at Chico State University. Mind you, I had barely passed the last one. I was visiting my girl-friend, Amber, at the Sports Page Bar where she was working. We'd been together for about six months. She ran the small place by herself; she would sneak glances at her schoolbooks between serving beers. Me? I was sneaking glances at her. It was worth the look.

It was a rather slow evening; I guess others were also doing that studying thing. Amber was really stressing with all her coursework, so I suggested she go home to study. After some hesitation, she agreed to let me fill in for her. I hopped over the bar. Well, walked around behind it. I had always wanted to bartend, but I never could seem to get hired. Here was my chance! No interview. No experience required. It was just a beer and wine joint. What could possibly go wrong?

The cash register was very simple, and ornately decorated—the old-school style where you just ring up the order, punching the numbers down. It would clang and show the numerical tally up top in a glass window, no computer BS. I barely charged anyone anyway. I hadn't really mastered the system. One thing I do remember is that there was an unfamiliar face planted at the bar. He was a short, over-weight guy with a mass of scraggly, unkempt hair falling over his face to his shoulders. He looked like the very untalented, inbred cousin of Ronnie Van Zant, the lead singer of Lynyrd Skynyrd.

Over the course of several beers (some of which might've even been paid for), I heard my first (and only) bartender/customer confession. The guy told me his story, of driving a truck all night and then trying to go to classes during the day. Thinking of Amber juggling the same type of work/school schedule, I developed a soft spot in my heart for this guy. For some reason, I wanted him to succeed. Maybe he'd name his firstborn after me: Ricky Van Zant.

As I closed out the one night of my life behind a bar, he asked if I could get him some amphetamines to help him through some of those tough hours. I briefly wondered why—if this guy was so sleep deprived, what the hell had he been doing sitting in this hole-in-the-wall and talking to me for the past three hours? Well, maybe I would've been smarter if I had spent more of my time studying. Instead, I felt empathy for this dude. And while I could not procure him any speed tablets, I did mention, while giddily wiping down my bar, that I could perhaps score him some cocaine.

At this point, in your mind, cut to a close-up of my face. Freeze the frame. Paint an arrow pointing at me and write the word *moron* on it. In flashing letters.

My new buddy, "Rod," readily agreed, and we two geniuses devised a plan. The agreement? The purchase by him of one quarter of a gram of cocaine from me. Yes, El Chapo, you heard me. One quarter of a gram. There are twenty-eight grams in one ounce. Sixteen ounces to one pound. Cocaine is usually transported over the border by the ton. That's two thousand pounds. Millions of dollars being exchanged. Me? I was about to earn the princely sum of twenty bucks.

Chapter 3: Freebird

The next morning, Rod showed up promptly at my place. To be honest, I had forgotten the exact details of our conversation the previous evening. Over the course of the next week, he would show up wherever Amber and I happened to be. It never occurred to me to wonder how this guy could be so omnipresent when his story was that he was always working or going to school. It seemed all he had time for was buying cocaine or amphetamine pills. We couldn't shake him.

But I didn't have any pills. I'd never taken speed pills. I didn't know what one would even look like. He had also asked about getting some cocaine. I didn't have any of that either—I was basically being a blowhard in my stint behind the bar that night.

After a week of relentlessly hounding us, Rod was able to catch each of us without the other—Amber and I had gotten into some sort of argument (not an uncommon occurrence by then) and had pledged one more time to end our relationship. It was during this time that Rod managed to buy twenty dollars of amphetamines from Amber. She had apparently acquired them from her boss at the Sports Page. I had no idea she was selling pills at work. I had no idea her that her boss, Don, the owner of the Sports Page, was providing her with these pills to sell. We really didn't know a lot about each other.

Meanwhile, I had decided to buy a little bit of cocaine to sell to Rod, mainly to rid myself of the guy. He was becoming a constant nuisance. This was before Nancy Reagan's "Just Say No" anti-drug program, so I guess I didn't get that if I just said "no," he'd eventually go away. Instead, I scored him his quarter gram.

Chapter 4: A Day in the Life

October 7, 1977.

Wow. We heard the news today. Oh boy.

Amber's boss, Don, had just been "busted" for selling an ounce of cocaine to a creepy degenerate who had been hanging around the Sports Page. And wouldn't you know? It turned out to be Rod. When had this pile of scum come up with the $2,000 to buy an ounce of coke from Don?

Actually, he hadn't. He was a CI, a confidential informant, for the Chico Police Department—our tax dollars were hard at work.

While this was going on, Chico State University had just been crowned the 1977 Number One Party School in America by *Playboy* magazine—that was the main reason I'd chosen this college in the first place. Unfortunately, Chico had the misfortune of being located in Butte County, California. Butte County, California, is a *very* conservative area—and they had decided to rid themselves of their dangerous drug epidemic.

Chapter 5: November Rain

Amber and I had both recently gotten hired at Madison Bear Garden, a fancy new bar/restaurant in town. She was a lunch-hour cocktail waitress, while I had landed the coveted job of Assistant Sandwich Preparer. The best part for me was when Amber would come up to my window and place an order. We'd flirt and smile. We were in pretty good spirits for having had such a festive Halloween the previous night. Maybe the cloud that had hung over us the past few weeks since Don's arrest was lifting. Perhaps they had only targeted him. Was the sword of Damocles being lowered? Would our heads be spared?

Just to put everything in perspective: Don had sold the cretin Rod an ounce of cocaine. Twenty-eight grams. I had sold him one quarter of a gram, over a hundred times less than Don. Amber had sold him some caffeinated pep pills.

Amber came up to my window—to place an order, I thought, until I saw the look on her face. "RICK. THEY ARRESTED ME!"

Behind her, I saw two conservatively dressed guys looming outside my food window. All I could think was, *Please let this be a great episode for* Candid Camera. *Please let us laugh about this and tell our grandchildren about the look on my face. Please let this be a great leftover from Halloween costume joke.*

After one of the unfamiliar faces behind her asked me if I was Richard Beren, I was 99 percent sure that this was not a joke. Only my mother called me "Richard," and that was when she was pissed at me, which was the majority of the first twenty years of my life. It was looking like she would be able to continue that streak for the next twenty.

When the other guy proudly produced a very poor Xerox (remember those?) of my license, even as my vision blurred, it became clear that I was fucked. I stepped out from behind the counter and heard my Miranda rights being read to me. Right at the fucking entrance. People were walking in and out of the restaurant.

"You are under arrest for the sale of amphetamines . . ." as I breathed out.

"And cocaine." Which caused me to suck my breath back in.

"Shit," I exhaled aloud.

I looked at Amber. She was literally trembling. I wanted to comfort her, but I couldn't—my hands were being cuffed behind my back. We squinted as we were led out into the bright fall afternoon. They covered the tops of our heads protectively so we wouldn't bump them as they eased us into the backseat of the patrol car. And with that, we drove off from our college life.

The younger of the two narcotics officers (who couldn't have been ten years older than I) seemed quite pleased with himself. "Yeah, we thought you two skipped town . . . we went by your house, and it looked like you had made a hasty exit. I guess we'll have to call off the APB," he said, chortling.

This guy's arrogance was making me carsick. I leaned over and whispered to Amber, "Don't say anything. We'll get a lawyer and get out of this."

Shell-shocked, she was only able to look forward and nod.

"What's that, big shot?" said the cop whose name I later learned was Pete Asilomar. He had been tasked with heading up Chico's newly established narcotics division. Now Detective Asilomar was hard at work attacking the amphetamine pipeline, one hundred pills at a time. (Now, of course, those same pills are legal and available at every corner Rite Aid across America. And in bulk at Costco.)

"Nothing," I answered.

"That's right. You're nothing, punk."

I surmised Detective Asilomar must've watched too many episodes of *Hawaii Five-O* (the original one). He was no McGarrett; his older partner (not Danno) even managed to groan.

The officers drove us through Chico, a place I had previously only associated with joy. It now seemed foreboding. All the buildings frowned down upon us, tsk-tsking with reproachful looks. People walking in the streets seemed so removed from us. How could they appear unfazed? Carry on with their lives? Couldn't they see the injustice taking place inside this automobile?

We arrived at the Chico Police Department, reminiscent of Mayberry R.F.D. We were ushered into separate but adjoining cells. Mine was replete with "Fester," the town drunk. No Barney Fife, though. The jail was over one hundred years old. Cattle rustlers had stood where I was right now. I promised myself to be cool for Amber, but before I could stop myself, I started pacing the three-by-six-foot space like a cow waiting to be slaughtered. My synapses struggled to connect. I knew I couldn't last more than five minutes in this place.

Okay. More than five minutes have passed, and you're still alive. Now I was wildly doing figure eights in my small space. Finally, Amber emerged—she had just spoken with a public defender. I rushed to the bars that separated us.

"Oh my God. What did he say?"

I was not the epitome of cool. She, on the other hand, seemed strangely calm. "We're going to the courthouse," she replied in a monotone. "I'm scared."

"Hang in there. I will never let anything happen to you." What I meant was worse than being arrested and locked up in jail.

My words dissipated through the cold iron bars. I wanted to tear them apart, like King Kong. You know, I actually tried to, to no avail.

An hour passed. Or was it a minute? There was no outside light, and no iPhone clocks inside. Jail time, like hospital time, was slow.

They gathered us up and moved us to the adjoining courtroom. I felt so impotent watching the girl I loved being herded into another cage. We were placed next to each other, but so far apart. Amber was alone. In my new cage, I was placed with a street-slick Black guy who had really gotten caught in the wrong town to be selling drugs. And he knew it. I imagine he was not the first Black man to be scared shitless in these chambers. People shifted in and out of the courtroom, the wheels of justice always churning. Each time the door opened, I'd longingly catch a glimpse of the placid world outside. (I experienced the same feelings in 1989 when I was under the trembling concrete concourse holding up three levels filled with fans right before the World Series in San Francisco during a massive earthquake. Panic underneath and within as I glanced outside the stadium at the serene bay. In each case, I wanted to be *out there*.)

"C'mon. Let's forget about all of this." I mean, what and who had I harmed? Rod had sought *me* out to buy the drugs. I didn't go looking for him. I didn't stand in front of an elementary school and peddle dope. I didn't even know where the elementary school in town was. I barely knew where my classes were. The world would not cease to spin if we were allowed to walk out these doors. I was basically a decent guy. Heck, I got that guy drugs because of his sob story—I had felt bad for him.

Continuing to deny my current reality, I rationalized even more. I was raised in Oakland, California, situated smack-dab in the middle of San Francisco and Berkeley. It is a very mixed and racially diverse town. I had an early introduction to different cultures, which I count as a blessing in my life. I became aware of my surroundings in the early sixties, when my elementary school was one of the first to integrate in the country. Oakland was also the headquarters of the Black Panther Party *and* the Hells Angels, who openly cruised around town. The politics were very liberal. I was there to witness hippies being tear-gassed at People's Park near UC Berkeley for protesting the war in Vietnam. I saw Huey Newton speak about civil rights on the steps of the Oakland-Alameda Courthouse. I saw the Summer of Love on Haight-Ashbury in San Francisco, and heard about the Hells Angels destroying it at the free Rolling Stones concert at Altamont, within ten miles of my home. Heck, I had lived next door to some of those "Angels" the previous summer.

Now, here I sat, in a jail. I had never been in a real jail cell before.

Amber and I awaited our turns in front of the judge. She was called first and released on her own recognizance, which meant she promised to return at a later date. Then it was my turn.

"Richard Beren?"

"Yes, sir," I answered the judge.

The charges made me sound like I had devoted half my life to the sale of drugs and narcotics, which was only half true. More mumbling and heavy breathing, all captured on the microphone in front of the judge. His heavy breaths sounded like the labored ones Neil Armstrong had taken when he stepped onto the moon. Hours passed. In reality, it was mere minutes. The judge cleared his throat and banged his gavel. As dangerous as I sounded, I was allowed back on the streets, promising to also return at a later date.

All right! Now I had to get cracking and right this sinking ship. We'd taken a blow. I felt like JFK must've while bobbing in the dark ocean after his PT boat had been rammed.

I found Amber crumpled in a heap in front of the courthouse by a stately hundred-year-old redwood tree. I sought her eyes. Our world had stopped. I would have to kick-start it like my very old, gasping-for-life, held-together-by-duct tape metallic green 1972 Honda CB350 motorcycle. I felt just about as powerful, and *its* battery had been dead for six months.

We traversed the formerly friendly college town streets. It was now dusk, my favorite time of day. This day, though, shadows from the fully mature oak trees loomed frighteningly over us, their crowns shuddering in judgment. A shiver of fall blew through the mostly empty streets as we silently walked the fifteen blocks or so to Amber's sister Brooke's house.

Brooke was home. She and her roommate had been drinking hot tea and studying by a warm fire—such a different afternoon than we had experienced. It was so tranquil. We were about to bust that up. We told them our story. At the end, there was complete silence. Disbelief. I remember that disbelief. I had experienced it about five hours earlier.

The streets were very dark as we staggered back to our place. Random bare tree limbs threatened to spear us with their branches now. Everything was closing in on us. It seemed around every blind corner, a hideous creature was about to catapult itself onto us, vomiting its condemnation. I was on a hallucinogenic trip. A bad one.

Chapter 6: Dirty Laundry

November 3, 1977. A few days later. Chico.

Dennis Lorimar's law office, 10:00 a.m. sharp. His offices were set in a beautifully restored Victorian mansion; we waited in the parlor, where, I imagined, many a young man these past 150 years had sweated out his prospective father-in-law's scrutiny as he had sought the daughter's hand. I felt just like one of those young men. I was waiting to be sized up. To present my case.

In burst Lorimar's secretary, Nancy. She was a bundle of energy and good vibes, and only a couple of years older than us. She seemed to grasp the ludicrousness of all this nonsense. Smiling widely, she brought us two steaming cups of coffee—very welcome, as this was pre-Starbucks—and told us her boss would be able to help us. Nancy professed that the sun rose and set with him.

Dennis Lorimar made his entrance, wearing a three-piece suit and looking every bit the young Clarence Darrow. Mr. Lorimar's large, meaty hand grasped mine. He had a friendly smile and a fleshy face that exuded confidence and warmth. I felt very good about this. Amber was inclined to go with a public defender—we had no money—but I believed we needed to take our best opportunity and thought Lorimar was it. We could worry about the money later. Lorimar had already successfully defended drug cases much larger than ours in town. Can you sell less than a quarter gram?

Behind Lorimar was his law partner, Jerry Kunkle. He also sported a three-piece suit, but was a small man with rather nondescript, proper features. They were both about thirty-five years old. They looked like the comedic magician act Penn & Teller. There were no jokes, but I hoped they could perform some magic. Lorimar got right down to business. He was very positive. We were too . . . for a moment.

"I've read the newspapers and seen you two on the ten o'clock news," he said.

I sensed rather than saw Amber's jaw drop. I stole a glance at her, and indeed, it had. "The news . . . on TV? Oh no," she moaned. It was news to me too, but I didn't want to exacerbate the drama, so I said nothing.

This was before constant 24-7 news programming. No such thing as the internet. No Facebook, Instagram, Twitter. No parents already hearing about this. We were 150 miles from them, a world away. Lorimar assumed we had known about the news on TV. He did not know, however, that we were trying to keep our parents in the dark. Amber had now completely lost any of the momentary confidence we'd previously experienced. This up-and-down roller coaster of emotions would be our constant for the next few months.

The two lawyers tried to put us at ease and agreed to take our case. As we left the offices, I put all my remaining energies into shoring Amber up. For a broke twenty-two-year-old guy, it was not easy to earn her faith.

"My parents are going to find out!" she cried.

I tried desperately to reassure her that would not happen, meanwhile knowing full well that I was one without knowledge.

Chapter 7: Feels Like the First Time

The next three weeks were a succession of minor ups and debilitating downs. Each time we turned around, there was another set of bad news. Money did not exist. Huge legal fees were outstanding. Classes became background noise. Life was mostly a dirge being played everywhere we were, sitting *shiva* (the Jewish tradition of seven days' mourning after a death) for almost a month. We were clinging to one another, hoping somehow this nightmare would go away. As a man (barely), I felt an extra burden of protecting and caring for a woman. I also felt responsible for putting Amber into this situation. I mean, I had met Rod that fateful night I filled in for her, and that was her very first time selling drugs. Can you imagine? First time! It's hard to believe. Plus, it had only happened because we were in a silly argument when the snitch came looking for me, so she had sold him pills instead of me. I didn't even know she had those things. What were the odds? No bookie in America would book them. Certainly not mine, and he's routinely pulverized me for the past twenty years.

Naturally, our romantic moments were full of stress and, unsurprisingly, not full of romance. Like . . . nothing was working, especially me. To top it off, I got fired from my job. I can't imagine how Bonnie and Clyde ever made love.

The noose was tightening. The lawyers were asking for money. I initially thought the entirety of the lawyers' fees would be $500. In actuality, it was more than ten times that. (This was 1970s' dollars, too.) The case was looking increasingly hopeless. I felt we were being railroaded into going whatever direction the district attorney wanted us to go.

Chapter 8: The Trial

December 5, 1977. A few weeks later.

Today, with friends supporting us, we would come face to face with our undercover narc, Rod, in court. I stood over him as he sat, silently glaring at him with murderous intentions, until my friend ushered me away. Amber and I were dressed in our collegiate best. I was in wide-wale cords and a gauze button-down shirt. My new Famolare "Get There" shoes (the ones with the wavy rubber soles) were laced up tight. Amber was in a calf-length jean skirt, a crisp blouse, and conservative, rubber-soled leather boots. We smelled as fresh as a Garden of Earthly Delights from sharing our Herbal Essences shampoo.

Rod. He was the best the county had to offer? He looked like a drug-addicted derelict. "Against type" casting, you might say. He mumbled, rubbed his nose with his threadbare Pendleton sleeve, and sniffed when asked if he would be willing to testify against us in the future. He agreed, which blew my mind. Our two lives were in the balance.

Now we stood in front of Judge Ann Haughlin, but our expensive attorney seemed to be invoking the right to remain silent. Maybe he was Teller, who famously has never spoken on stage. I was flabbergasted. Even the judge questioned him to see if he was certain he didn't want to at least say something in our defense. Judge Haughlin seemed motherly to me—a confused and disappointed mother at this point, but empathetic and kind. It seemed like she wanted to give us an out. We'll never know. Kunkle never gave her the opportunity.

This was not good. Earlier the free public defender had asked the court to dismiss similar cases for his clients, cases which had also involved this modern-day Judas. I decided I needed to sneak out of the fort to get the cavalry.

Chapter 9: Oops! . . . I Did It Again

December 7, 1977. On the road to Oakland.

A date that will live in infamy. In no way do I want to compare my plight to that of the brave men and women of Pearl Harbor, but it was ironic that I was hurtling past the World War II mothball fleet in the Carquinez Strait as I made my way down the 165-mile drive from Chico to Oakland. There was no traffic. You always get to places you don't really want to go in record time.

"What's wrong?" my mom asked.

"Nothing, Mom," I lied. "Can't a guy visit his parents?"

The last time I had pulled up to their house in the middle of the semester was when a dear friend of mine had died on the way back to school from Christmas break. I had cried in my mother's arms (the first time ever) on their couch for hours. This was about to happen again. For now, she announced that she'd go to the store and cook my favorite dinner. She left me rambling around the empty house. Memories (mostly screams of terror) filled my thoughts. How could I do this to these people?

I must've dozed off. When I awakened, it was to my father peeking his head into my room. He had a grin from ear to ear. He was an eternal optimist, clearly where I'd inherited this trait from. He was also smart—I wish that gene had come through. He was standing tall and trim with a full head of perfectly coiffed silver hair. To this day, he's successful and always dresses the part, down to his Ferragamo shoes. He looks good and knows it. Even so, he'll ask you to tell him many times throughout any given day.

We hugged, and I kissed him. When I stepped back to look at him, he read the pain in my eyes. I would see the same in his two hours later.

"Come back and talk to me," he said encouragingly.

I watched my father shed his beautiful clothes. He easily slipped into an equally stylish, comfortable outfit. *I hope he won't mind shitting himself in those*, I thought to myself. Obviously, I'd driven the nearly two hundred miles here with a huge weight on my shoulders. A small pep talk would not fix this one.

We walked toward the front of the house. Dinner smelled so damn great. Too bad I would no longer have an appetite. Soon no one would.

"C'mon, Rick. You've never been able to shake me up. God knows, you've tried."

We reached the kitchen, and I saw my mom shoot my dad a hopeful look. He shook his head. It wasn't that I was in trouble with a girl. Well, it was. But it wasn't what they were thinking. I had always pushed the envelope of irresponsible behavior. I was never mean or destructive. More mischievous and rebellious . . . I guess because I had this envelope of protection and support. This episode would eclipse them all.

"I'll have a drink," proclaimed my father.

We adjourned to the bar. After I suggested we take our drinks to the living room, my dad eased into his favorite big chair. My mom sat on the hearth next to him, in front of a roaring fire I had carefully constructed. I felt like diving headfirst into it. Instead, I was about to burn them. I sat on the couch across from them both.

"Here's to good health," my dad offered.

"Good health," we responded, and I pulled down a large slug of Chivas Regal. Only the best for me. I deserved warm horse piss with foam on top, swirling in a shit-rimmed glass. It burned my throat and passed the lump in my heart. As I breathed back out, the tears started pouring down my face.

What a shit I was. This was not a cute little Ricky misdeed. Some-times those (after the proper amount of time had passed) left my father shaking his head and making a humorous aside at my "imagination." No. This was major *tsuris* (Yiddish for *trouble*, a word with which I was not unfamiliar). I noticed I wasn't the only one taking a large gulp of fine scotch.

"Well," I began.

Then, with a lot of hemming and hawing (and no editorializing), I managed to bring them sadly up to date. For some stupid fucking reason, I found myself laughing at the end of the story. They must've thought I was nuts. Or maybe they thought (fantasized) that it was some sort of sick fraternity hazing prank to pull on one's parents. I guess I was just so overwhelmed with containing my emotions for the past month that my brain's prefrontal cortex got confused, and laughter emerged. The fire did not seem to warm the cockles of my mother's heart at all. She sat there frozen, yet mere inches from the flames. I'm sure that among the many thoughts that flooded her brain was, what in God's name would she be able to tell her friends at the tennis club?

My parents knew I was no stranger to drugs. They knew I smoked pot. I had even puffed a joint in front of my dad when it got passed to me in our limo on the way to the Super Bowl, when the (forever) Oakland Raiders demolished the Vikings in January 1977. When it came around to me again, my dad had said, "*Genug* with the pot, Rick" —Yiddish that can be loosely translated to "enough already." I'm pretty sure that's the first time "genug" and "pot" have been used together in a sentence.

But the word "cocaine" had taken the air out of the room. The fire almost extinguished itself. When I finished, the room was silenced for a full, awkward minute. It might never have ended but for a thunderous clap from that brilliant fire I had made. I sure did know how to torch things. This seemed to startle my parents back to focus. We sat there inside a fog that matched the murk hovering just outside on the East Bay Hills, well known for capturing the world-famous fog off the San Francisco Bay.

I looked up for the first time since I had begun talking an hour earlier. I was greeted by two vacant stares. My parents' eyes were as drained as their skin. My father spoke first.

"I just don't understand how you can be so fucking stupid," he, in all fairness, opened with.

I think he was just wearily thinking out loud. My mother silently concurred. As I continued to share more details, he could only respond with winces. "I thought you had learned your lesson about this."

Yes—this was the *second* time I had been caught selling drugs.

The first time had been when I was working at my high school's version of Arnold's coffee shop from *Happy Days*. Ours was an ice cream parlor, though. About ten of my high school buddies also worked at the Creamery. I had graduated from high school and was attending the local junior college. Boy, was I on an upward fast track.

Leanne, my then-girlfriend, was in her senior year of high school. We had been together all her high school years, and her senior prom was to take place that weekend. The Creamery was busy, all the guys and girls there excited for the festivities. We were scooping ice cream out of the front and slinging plastic sandwich bags of pot out of the back. ("Lids," if you can recall what they were called. Ten dollars for a healthy four-finger lid.)

I had sold a lid to one of the dishwashers. He was a young, Native American, long-haired, regular guy. A fairly regular transaction, or so I thought. *Thought* being the operative word here—thought seemed to be what I had given little of regarding the direction of my life.

Well, it seems my good buddy, the dishwasher guy, had previously been arrested for possession of marijuana. Remember, this was 1974 . . . before every block in California had a marijuana dispensary. So having, and especially selling, marijuana was a thing. I suppose I was just a bit before my time. A visionary, if you will. Unfortunately, and unbeknownst to me, Carlos had turned on me and agreed to set up a purchase with me in order to receive a more lenient charge.

After my shift ended at midnight, I had made my way to the very desolate rooftop of the mall parking structure, along with a coworker I'd magnanimously offered a ride home. As soon as I'd arrived at my 1972 Vega hatchback, I'd heard screeching tires and saw four cars racing toward me. They'd surrounded me with what seemed like a dozen shouting voices. I'd heeded the command to "put my hands in the air." Blinded by powerful flashlights searing my eyes, I'd still managed to make out the large revolvers pointed at my head. When they say guns look bigger when they are pointed at you, they're not kidding. These had looked like those cannons on a destroyer cruising the Atlantic Ocean coming upon a little fishing trawler.

Frankly, I was greatly relieved when they screamed an announcement that they were "the police!" This was Oakland, after all, and not even the marginally safe part of it.

This was a ride my coworker would not soon forget. It took a bit of effort, but after I was handcuffed, I managed to emphatically tell the cops that she had nothing to do with any of this. See? Aren't I just your friendly ice-cream-and-marijuana merchant? Fortunately, they let her go. I don't think she slept much that night—she had turned as white as the whipped cream on our old-fashioned French vanilla when the guns came out. She did manage to call our boss, and he in turn called my parents. He was a good guy, and that couldn't have been a good call.

At the station, I'd been led into a small interrogation room just like the ones you see on TV. Small table. Wooden chairs. Coppers on one side. Me on the other. No cigarettes. No Coke cans. They wanted me to give up the guy who sold to me. This was a problem. He was a friend. I felt it wasn't he who had fucked up. I don't even think the act of selling pot was such a fuck-up. And it wasn't even forty years hence. See? I'm a friendly drug dealer with ethics and foresight.

My main concern was that this was the beginning of a three-day holiday, and Leanne's senior prom was the next night. I stupidly asked them how long I'd be incarcerated and shared my concerns for the prom. They said that if I didn't help them with this information, I'd not get out "for days."

I hemmed and I hawed. They wanted me to go to my friend and make a purchase. All the while, they would be monitoring the entire event. I just couldn't see myself buying pot with the knowledge that I'd be getting my friend into a big mess . . . like the one I was in right now. I wouldn't rat. It was awful, but I declined to help these coppers.

"I won't do it," I declared. "I can't."

The two police officers had left me there to stew. No food. No water or bathroom. How long? I don't know. No clocks. It's not like I deserved any great treatment. I felt horrible.

Right on cue, in came the bad cop. He did his best to make me feel even worse. I felt like such a loser already, so it would take a professional to reduce me even further—and he was a pro, just like you see on every *Law and Order* episode. Now I was getting rattled around pretty good. It wasn't a fair fight. Two pros vs. a moron. A teenage one at that.

Now the nice cop entered and whispered into the ear of the Oakland Police dick. (I'll use that term in reference to the nicknames bestowed upon detectives. It also describes what this guy truly is.) "Dick" slammed his hand down on the table and announced, "Shit. Your father is here. And he's with Stan Golde."

Ah, Judge Stan Golde, my dad's best friend and Cal Berkeley Jewish fraternity brother. The guys in the white hats had arrived!

Now, I don't advocate selling drugs—a lesson it took me a couple of times to learn. But if you're gonna do it, do it in a city where your dad is connected and has many high-powered friends. The quick version? I had been allowed to immediately walk, I hadn't had to talk, *and* I got to take Leanne to the senior prom. We just didn't have any pot to smoke that night. Well . . . none of mine.

It hadn't all been rosy. I did have to greet my dad and Judge Golde at 3:00 a.m. in the downtown Oakland Police Jail. This was quite unpleasant for everyone involved, to say the very least. Jewish parents (like all parents) thrive on being proud of their children *and* being able to brag about them ad nauseum. For Jews, it's an art form. They have a word for it in Yiddish: *kvelling*. There'd been no kvelling from my father that night. I'd vowed to make him be able to kvell over me one day, profusely apologizing and promising to live the straight and honorable life from there on out.

Luckily, Judge Golde (Uncle Stan, as we sometimes referred to him) had seen so much worse that he'd assured my dad that what I had done wasn't exactly on par with capital murder. I did find out much later that Stan's initial recommendation to my distraught dad was to let me rot in jail overnight to scare the shit out of me—under "watchful eyes," of course.

Certainly I was far too stupid to understand how fortunate I had been—now I had the proof. My "get out of jail free" card had been punched. Fool me once, shame on you. Fool me twice, I'm a fucking idiot. How stupid was I, to actually sell drugs to an undercover asshole twice?!

Chapter 10: Tomorrow Never Knows

I awakened the next morning with the fervent hope that last night had all been a bad dream. It *was* a bad dream. But it was also real.

I went into the kitchen. I had heard my parents in there, and hoped when I got in there that they'd tell me to leave and never darken their doorstep again. What I experienced was the opposite. I found two people united in love and support for me.

My mom came to me, hugged me, and said, "We love you."

My dad told me he would do everything he could and "stand beside me through to the end."

It was like I was running for Congress instead of from the law.

I could and I couldn't believe this. I managed to feel good *and* so much worse than ever before. My parents had just stepped up and hit one out of the ballpark. Not that I deserved it. I was a worthless thorn in their side. Jewish guilt—ah, she's a powerful seductress. I promised to turn into a rose one day. With more hope than confidence, they agreed with me on that.

"First, we have to address this situation," my dad declared.

We called the attorneys in Chico. There were speakerphones, no FaceTime. I watched and listened (on one end only) to my father, who was quite experienced in complicated international business negotiations, as he dealt with these country bumpkin lawyers. It was painful. He was resigned to following their lead.

Still, that wouldn't stop him from lining up the troops. Next, he called his best friend, Uncle Stan (good ol' Superior Court Judge Stanley Golde), to bring him up to speed. Round Two. (Not 2.0. That term didn't exist yet.) He was also close to our state senator, Nicolas Petris, and told my attorneys so. I felt so much love for him. I ached to make him proud of me.

The attorneys in Chico suggested that heavy artillery fired from afar might create a larger mess. They assured my dad that they had a handle on the local politics and how the system was best served in their town. They also wanted $3,000 right away. Our entire home in the nicest part of town had only cost $30,000 a few years earlier. My dad would now go on to pay for Amber's and my defense—and he hadn't even met Amber yet.

My father went to work. He was happy there. He had full control of his life while in his office domain. I hung out with my mom, then took a walk in the Oakland hills with my dog and Brian, my best friend from high school. He was going to law school. I was approaching the law from a different vantage point. The view of the Bay from the Oakland hills was astonishing, as usual. We were surrounded by a forest of redwood trees and looked out onto the San Francisco skyline and the Golden Gate Bridge. I visualized this view often during the next few months.

Later, I had a very quiet dinner with my parents—one where you heard every scrape of the silverware and gulp of the throat. Our inner thoughts rendered us silent. Mine screamed for me to get back to Chico. I was ready to begin the fight anew with my new reinforcements. My parents feared Chico. No longer a friendly little college town, it now represented an area poised to lock their son away in its jail.

Chapter 11: Imagine

The next morning, I woke up early to head back to Chico. Before I left, I assured my parents that I would refrain from doing anything stupid. Or stupid-er. I mean, the bar was low. How could I do anything dumber?

I promised to run the other way if I saw anyone partake of any drugs. This being the late seventies, and me in the midst of a rambunctious college setting, that would prove to be difficult. It would've been difficult to avoid cocaine in a *church* in those days. Maybe even in the confessional.

When I got back, I found Amber in bed. Walker, my dog, burst through the door and jumped on her and Rusty, her dog. Amber was a combination of relief and anger. "Oh, hon! Where were you? I was so worried!"

I saw that she had slept fitfully. It had been forty days and forty long nights now since we had been arrested. It seemed everywhere I went, I caused my loved ones angst. I would've done anything to erase her misery. I would've gone to prison for five years to spare them this agony. (Ahem. Well. Maybe not five years.)

I hopped into the warm bed as fast as my little legs would allow. "Oh, you think you can just barge in here with those icicle fingers and I'm gonna start moaning and groaning for you, huh? You're not James Bond, buster." I was more like Jimmy Bond, played by Woody Allen. I furiously tried to warm my hands. Our dogs raced in and around the one-room shack. There was a gnashing of hair, teeth, legs, and bodies, a frantic free-for-all. It may not have seemed romantic when you opened your eyes and saw dogs and people panting in equal proximity to your face, but it was the best way I could have imagined. And I would imagine it a lot.

Minutes later, Amber's sister Brooke stopped by. We feigned nonchalance, but with the bed askew and everyone asunder, it was obvious what had been going on. Yes, either we had either just made love or I had beaten the shit out of her. Amber probably would've preferred the latter.

We gathered, and I told them the details of my visit with my parents. We all agreed that my parents were amazing. I was telling the girls of the pain on my parents' faces when I noticed a similar look on Amber's.

"This is a positive thing," I stressed.

She was sobbing heavily now. "I just want to be able to tell my parents," she wept. "You get to lean on yours for comfort and support. Who do I get to lean on?"

"Me" was not a very good answer. I felt quite infantilized. I experienced that a lot. I would've been unable to provide strength without the help of my parents. I felt twelve. I had no control of anything in my life. Well, maybe about as much control as a twelve-year-old boy would. Well, about as much as one reading his first *Playboy* magazine.

I imagined what it would have been like if we hadn't had this burden weighing us down. We could've been having a nice, normal college relationship. It could have included all the regular ups and downs of young love. Maybe it could have had a natural beginning, middle, and end. Instead, while everything and everyone carried on frivolously around us, we lived in misery. Imagine.

Chapter 12: Just Remember I Love You

New Year's Eve! Hallelujah! Finally, the end had come to quite the shit-filled year. You've got to agree—I mean, I had met a girl I'd really fallen for, and six months later, we just kept falling.

Our plan had us celebrating at the hippest place in town. The coolest band would be performing. They were known for their mean *Star Wars*–themed boogie; they also played the newest disco tunes that were the current rage. Thinking about that, we felt good for a moment. We escaped our heads briefly, and actually behaved like two normal twenty-two-year-old college students. That meant we were still in bed, and it was dusk.

When we finally hit the club, Amber glimmered in her shimmery lime-green miniskirt, while I must say I felt resplendent in my colorfully stitched bell-bottom jeans and two-toned platform shoes. We danced a lot that night. Bred and raised in Oakland, even though I'm white, I couldn't help having been infused with a bit of Oaktown soul. I had embraced this hip sound. Oh yeah, I'm cool. White cool.

Laughter! Music! Love! I had forgotten those foreign emotions. At 3:00 a.m., I found myself slow-dancing in the middle of the room with Amber in my arms. We swayed to the song "Just Remember I Love You" by Firefall. But mostly, we just stood there and clung to each other.

"I love you," I whispered into her ear.

It was kind of the first meaningful time one of us had said that. We hadn't really gone through the natural process of being able to do that one simple thing. Amber pressed her head into my neck and chest harder. If we held on tightly together like this, maybe they wouldn't be able to break us apart. I resolved to do everything in my feeble powers to get this girl out of this mess.

"I made a resolution," I told her.

"What?" She pulled back and looked straight into my eyes.

When we separated a few inches, the cold air rushed between us.

"That I love you and it'll be forever, just like the song."

1977 was over, and good riddance.

Chapter 13: New Year's Day

I was barely able to open one eye at a time, to a sight that left no doubt in my mind that either the night before had been fantastic, or we had survived a hostile siege.

The aching in my head had been hard earned—a good old-fashioned hangover induced only by alcohol. Focused on coordinating my eyelids to blink in syncopation, I sat up and reviewed my surroundings. Sprawled in the corner lay for all intents and purposes two deceased dogs. Next to me was a body, its face buried in the pillow. I didn't know if it was breathing. I thought and I hoped it was Amber—if not, this would look bad for me in court.

Staggering over to make some coffee. I tripped over the entwined dogs, who barely acknowledged my existence. "Great watchdogs," I muttered.

Then it crept up on me like the Blob. This wasn't a creepy dream. The change of year hadn't changed anything. We were still being actively prosecuted by the Butte County justice system. I tried three times to outfox my beleaguered brain, to try to verify what was the reality. Well, this bad dream was the reality.

"Fuck. I can't even enjoy my fucking hangover."

My eyes wandered over the counter strewn with debris. There I found a note.

"I love you too," it said.

Chapter 14: Truckin'

"Mr. Arnold Gustine?" I stepped up to the opaque-faced receptionist seated at a typewriter in front of an equally dull, pea-green wall.

"Please have a seat. Mr. Gustine is expecting you."

Butte County probation offices. I turned around and spotted a dozen circa-1960s, very uncomfortable-looking plastic modular chairs bolted together in the adjacent waiting area.

Amber checked in and was immediately ushered back to see her probation officer. She barely had time to pace or fret. We crossed our fingers at each other as she was led down the grim hallway.

Then it became just me, alone in this bare waiting space. I was nervous, mainly for Amber—my story was what it was. I sat. I paced. There were a few issues of *Boys' Life* from several years earlier strewn about. They were dusty, their pages greasy from the undoubted hundreds of nervous parolees who had thumbed through the dated articles.[1]

I read several articles in one *Boys' Life* magazine—two, actually, my first and last. It was not a magazine for this boy's life. I shifted uncomfortably and moved from chair to chair. No discernible emotions emanated from the receptionist behind the tabletop. In fact, the steel desk had more movement than the lady sitting behind it. I had just

---

1   Why is it that the waiting rooms with the longest waits always have the worst magazines? Meanwhile, in other rooms, a current magazine library is spread out in front of you, and maybe even a cool aquarium—your ass barely hits the seat (usually a comfortable one, at that) before you're immediately ushered in to see whoever it is you're there to do whatever you gotta do with.

skimmed an article titled "How to Resuscitate a Person" and wondered if it might come in handy, unless she had already passed.

Thirty minutes later, out came Mr. Gustine. He entered from as bleak an area as the one I resided in. I was disappointed on so many levels. I had hoped the delay would've included a hostage situation in the back; at least then I could have tripped up the gunman and saved the day. I'd be rewarded with a handshake, my file ripped in half. But no, this man had just been pulling an old-fashioned Napoleonesque little-man power move and had kept me waiting.

Gustine. I was introduced to a short and squinty-eyed being with wire-rimmed glasses. He had prematurely thinning hair combed over one half of his head. He may have been thirty-five, but he looked closer to fifty-five—he must have looked fifty since he had been twenty. He had a goatee (which has never looked good on anyone) that mostly hid his acne-pocked face. It formed a point, which I was to learn came from how often he stroked it with his spindly little fingers. This also caused it to be greasy, giving him the look of a hefty, sleazy little devil-man. Gustine was outfitted in cheap knock-off Wallabee shoes with white crew socks that were on full display, his khaki pants being a good three inches too short, held up by an overworked belt trying to corral a bulging waistline. At his thighs, the pleats were strained flat and threadbare, worn from being rubbed by sweaty palms.

He extended his hand, offering no apologies for the wait. I was here to get along with this guy. I knew full well that his reports held an inordinate amount of influence with the judge, and he knew it too. This was the way the system was designed in Butte County. There is a word for someone, usually in an inferior position, who is able to temporarily be in charge of someone who would normally be in the authoritative position. (I learned this word while playing the game Balderdash with my future wife Carole and her best friend Laura, who created it.) That word is *satrap*. Gustine was a satrap for the moment, a subordinate official who held power over others at a particular moment in their life, and he relished his satrapy.

After we shook hands—his palm was moist—Gustine led me down a narrow corridor into a very cramped office. I wondered where Amber was and how things were going for her. As I sat down and looked around, a little smile crossed my mouth. His office walls were plastered with billboards of the Grateful Dead! The Dead were the poster child band for drugs and rock 'n' roll—Bay Area gods, with a following almost cult-like, and mostly always supremely high. This couldn't be bad.

Is this guy cool? I wondered. *Has Ricky managed to slip one past the system again?*

Was I going to skate?

I immediately brought up to Gustine that I had been to many of the shows depicted on the walls. Bill Graham was the Dead's manager, for God's sakes. His Winterland Ballroom in San Francisco was where I practically lived during my teen years. The Dead were as close to a house band as you got. We were so lucky to grow up in a time and place where we could experience, in person, all this amazing music, not to mention the accompanying cosmic light shows. It wasn't lost on me that I was here discussing a drug arrest amidst placards of the place where I had imbibed many drugs. You'd have been hard-pressed to find someone at any of those shows who wasn't high.

I thought I had stumbled on a kindred spirit here. I should've stopped thinking. It's overrated.

Gustine grunted and squeezed himself behind his government-issued metal bureau. There were a few law journals scattered about an otherwise empty shelf. The books focused on crime and punishment from the 1950s. Clearing his throat, he shuffled my case file papers in front of him; he squinted and pushed his glasses back up on his nose, looked at me, and began a well-rehearsed interview.

He made sure to ask me for clarification if he didn't (or pretended not to) understand my answers. He said he wanted to write down exactly what I told him. In the folder were letters mailed from family friends. One was from my dad's best friend, the judge. Another was from Senator Petris. They weren't trying to bully Gustine, but to gently influence him. They knew that putting their names out there as a favor to my father would put Gustine in the position of receiving a favor from them in the future. Quid pro quo. A term made famous some fifty years later by someone who should do jail time.

Our inquisition ended after about forty-five minutes. They were long minutes, but I felt I had presented myself well. I readily acknowledged that I had made an error in judgment. I agreed (after he brought it up) that this wasn't the first time, either. *Dang—I hoped that earlier arrest was erased from my record.* I realized some amount of punishment, although not preferred, would be understandable.

Gustine stroked his slimy goatee (for maybe the hundredth time). Then he leaned forward, straining the springs in his clearly overworked chair. "All of this is *bullshit.*"

He slammed the file down as he spat the words out at me. My head jerked back a bit, and I went to the two-minute drill. My eyes grew as wide as they had been in many weeks—and it had been a few eye-opening weeks. The room began to close in on me. Those once-friendly signboards now seemed as sinister as the man sitting in front of them. He began asking me ridiculous questions, as if we were in a *Dragnet* or *Perry Mason* episode. Turns out (I ascertained along the way) Gustine was a frustrated lawyer, cop, and now perhaps B-level actor. I believed he was a very frustrated man.

I had to get out of there before things really got out of hand. He was getting lathered up—I thought I detected a bit of saliva formed at the cracks of his bearded, dry mouth. He launched into a litany of reasons that I, my father, my girlfriend, and a host of other factors had molded me into his declarations of "what is wrong with society"; I nodded, agreed to this diatribe, and, when the opportunity presented itself, politely asked if there was "anything else I can help you with." He waved me off with disdain, and I hightailed it out of there.

Amber was waiting for me in the car, the little ashtray slid all the way out and stuffed with cigarette butts. She had been out there for over an hour. She had gotten along quite well with her probation officer—he had practically apologized to her for her case being so seemingly blown out of proportion—and figured that my interview had also gone famously. She thought that since I had been in there for so long (she didn't know I had waited for a half hour to see Gustine), "you guys were best friends."

"It was *fucked*," I told her and lit a cigarette.

"What?" she gasped, reaching for my smoke.

Here again, we had been optimistic for a moment, then brought crashing back down into a fresh new hell for the rest of the day.

Amber's PO had plotted out a very minor punishment. He outlined a fifteen-day sentence which would include a work-and-school-release program. This would allow her to go to classes and then on to work afterwards. She'd be able to schedule work every night and basically just sleep at the jail. She might possibly have to spend only one night locked up, with the rest being time served for good behavior. It still sounded onerous to us, but tenable—especially now that Gustine had cavalierly tossed around "one year in the county jail with no work or school release privileges" for me, much like the nickel tips I'd later hear he was known for.

We drove the twenty miles back to Chico in silence. The only noise was the rattle from my 1974 convertible Karmann Ghia's engine as the wind rushed past. The cold, pouring rain that leaked on us from the ripped top after the recent car stereo theft did not lighten our moods. We could only wait.

Chapter 15:

"The Waiting" Is the Hardest Part

January 7, 1978. A few long days later.

Tom Petty was right.

Amber's report finally arrived. It came in an official-looking packet from the Butte County probation office. We unsealed the manila envelope and tore through the ten-page document to find that her probation officer had called for a small period of detention—perhaps only two days! He further stated she was an excellent candidate for the much-desired work-and-school-release program. The report also said she had been the brains of the operation, which *really* confused me, but I guess that's why I wasn't the brains of the operation.

The mail for me, however, had not arrived. As we waited, we wondered about what it could contain with great speculation. Would it be similar?

"No news is good news. Hope for the best and expect the worst," and several other clichés became my mantra . . . until they weren't.

Several anxiety-riddled days later, Gustine called. He knew I had to have seen Amber's dispatch by now. I could've recited it to him word for word. He also knew that I was hoping for a similar review. Then he told me there were just a few tiny little things he wanted to clear up with me before he could, "in all good conscience," submit his summary. He said I would have to come see him again in person one more time.

Damn. This could not bode well. He had shown me at our first meeting that he was a sneaky bastard and not to be trusted—now what could he want?

Chapter 16: Smiling Faces Sometimes

January 10, 1978. A few more long days later.

I drove to the Butte County Courthouse probation offices alone. When I got there, it was a completely different story. As I entered with trepidation, Gustine greeted me immediately and obsequiously with open arms. He sported a sickly grin and seemed very self-satisfied. Maybe he *had* just satisfied himself. Or he may have just eaten. His thighs scraped against each other as he waddled me back to his office; I watched and wondered how his ass cheeks struggled to compete for space in his pants with his shirt tucked in there too. His stomach had given up, and he appeared ready to give birth. He looked like a fully dressed mini sumo wrestler.

"What can I answer for you, sir?" I asked in as upbeat a way as possible upon entering his office. I wasn't a good actor, but I gave this my best performance, wearing my false optimism on my sleeve. I wanted this to be quick and clean.

Wheeling around, he shot out, "Cut the shit, motherfucker!" I knew he was loving every moment of my body flinching as he closed his office door.

This was not a safe place.

We sat down. "How do you like being spoken to like that?" he asked in a singsong voice.

I kept quiet. He was actually frightening me.

"You are so full of shit, and I am going to make sure I see your pretty face in prison. You know what they do to pretty boys like you?" He had become visibly excited. Without ease, he rose from his chair. He crept toward me and leaned into my ear, whispering now.

"They will take you to a dark and dank soundproof room far off, where nobody can see, hear, or give a shit about you, and five or six of the biggest guys in the joint will fuck you until they get tired of your pretty ass," he hissed.

I sat motionless. As he briefly turned away, I managed to sneak a quick peek down at my butt. It wasn't bad. Nothing special.

"Then, when they're done, they will send you out into the general population for the rest to do whatever they feel like doing to you." He sucked in some air, so worked up now he was perspiring. "Or you may get lucky, and one huge stud may claim you and declare you are his. Make you his sole bitch."

He huffed and he puffed. He was the Big Bad Wolf.

"Oh no. You won't cross anyone, because they will shank your face into a dozen cute pieces."

His stubby arms had gotten into the act, slicing through the air near my face while he talked. He only stopped to theatrically caress my cheek. I became nauseated with him hovering so close to me; it was impossible not to be overwhelmed by his sweat, breath, and very cheap cologne mixture. As I mouth-breathed, struggling to avoid this horrific trifecta, his leg pressed against my shoulder. My mind went blank and raced at the same time. I mean, look. I was twenty-two. Most faces were at their prettiest at that age. I agreed with him on that evaluation.

"Your father won't be able to do a fucking thing for you, either. No matter how much influence he's got. That doesn't matter on the inside, when your asshole is staring a lifer in the face day in and day out."

Gustine spat these words out so viciously and so close to me that I caught some leftover corn on my pretty face. I'm not all that quick, but I was getting the picture. Oh yeah, I figured it out. Gustine resented the close relationship I enjoyed with my father. He hated my dad's money, and I'm thinking he was not a fan of the Jewish religion, either. I was just guessing, but one thing was pretty certain: he did not much like anything about me.

"You'd be wise to think about a few things, Richard," he said, stroking my shoulder-length hair. "I am going to make it so you never see that cunt again."

With that, I pushed his hand away, standing and wheeling to face him with more hatred than I had ever felt toward another person.

"C'mon, Richard." He stepped even closer and lowered his voice again. "There are ways you can get out of this."

He stretched out his flabby arms from his V-neck, armless sweater-vest. What was this guy's game? Besides being fascinated with my derriere? I maintained my cool. I clearly wanted to physically anni-hilate him, but I didn't think that would serve me very well, besides feeling fantastic.

"Get the fuck away from me." I had raised my voice.

This surprised and halted him. Maybe the comatose receptionist had heard me. Regardless of why, Gustine snapped out of his trance-like mode, taking inventory of his surroundings. "What, Richard? What are you shouting about?" he asked in a singsong voice as he peeked toward the door. "I was only attempting to warn you of things you may have to be careful about."

He scuttled back behind his desk.

"Oh, sure." I brightened up. Then I asked him, "Then why don't you see to it that I never go through a situation like that?"

"I like you, Richard. But you don't see the big picture here."

God, I really hated it when people called me "Richard." Or when they said "big picture here." But I wasn't about to tell him that, or *anything* more about myself.

Gustine's breathing had slowed now. He mopped the sheen from his forehead. "Get out of here if you will not give me any information as to where you obtained your drugs."

I wouldn't do that. I got caught. I was stupid. If I gave up the guy who had sold me the drugs just to save myself, I would be no better than that whore Rod.

I scrambled to leave. Just as I grabbed the doorknob, though, I heard, "Oh, Richard?"

It froze me in my tracks. He reminded me of slimy Jabba the Hutt. I didn't want to turn around and face him. If I had, I just may have vomited on his tiny Jabba desk.

"When you get to Vacaville, your approach is not going to work," he said with a smile. Then he sniffed, snorted, and chortled like the swine he was and shuffled a few papers, barely able to stifle the grin behind his stringy mustache. I left.

Vacaville?! What the fuck is he talking about, Vacaville? That is a god-damned California state prison! Charles Manson and Sirhan Sirhan are fucking imprisoned there. Murderers. Assassins.

I staggered out of the offices and into my car. In a daze, I found myself back at Amber's place. I told her my experience blow by blow. At the end, we sat quietly on the edge of the bed.

"I'm proud you held out," she finally said softly.

"Yeah. He was pretty fine," I mumbled.

"No, I mean the other stuff. You know. Your father and money and your religion . . . and me." We locked eyes with one another at that last comment. "I know these are all sensitive subjects for you," she added.

"Well, he didn't bring up my dog, so I was able to maintain my cool," I weakly joked.

My father would be a constant source of support. He was fully consumed with trying whatever he could to help us. This often found him writing passionate letters to Gustine citing my redeeming qualities (which tested his creativity), or phoning him several times a week to try to sway him toward a more lenient recommendation. Gustine often left my dad on hold for twenty minutes or more, then curtly brushed him off moments after he picked up the phone. My father always kept his cool. He *was* cool.

Chapter 17: Folsom Prison Blues

January 14, 1978. Just a couple of days later.

My report arrived. Whatever my dad and I had done was to no avail. The wording was terse. It included some interesting terms to describe me. One was that I was Amber's "mule"—just the underling carrying out Amber's big drug-cartel operation. This didn't make much sense to me. Wasn't this her first drug sale? And she already had a mule?! Or was I missing something?

Gustine recommended that I spend three years in state prison. I didn't know whether to laugh or cry. So I did both.

Chapter 18: Lawyers, Guns and Money

February 18, 1978. A long few weeks later.

Our first day to argue in court arrived just a little over a year after I had met Amber outside a frat party. Happy anniversary! Time does fly by when you're having fun. If you were watching this story play out on TV with the sound off, you'd think we were young Republicans off to a Ronald Reagan rally, and Rod was the degenerate drug pusher.

Amber and I sat there silently while the greasy witness for the prosecution, Rod, got the chance to speak his well-rehearsed lines. It was infuriating. Then it was time for our attorney to offer his kick-ass defense rebuttal—but yet again, he sat there like a mime. A resting one. Not one word.

We were being remanded back for sentencing on March 29. This would be our only opportunity to plead our case. As we exited, I stopped Kunkle.

"Why didn't you say anything?" I implored.

He looked at me quizzically. "Just because you paid an attorney, do you want preferred treatment?"

"Yes! Yes! That's exactly what I want!"

Amber's initial idea of procuring a public defender now seemed like a good one. At least then you can't complain about what you're getting for your money.

Chapter 19: Long Train Runnin'

February 20 – March 28, 1978.

There were train tracks right outside the Sports Page. The trains would slow down while switching directions. I just wanted to hop on one and go wherever it took me. Had to be a better place than this.

Easter vacation arrived, and we went home to our respective parents' houses. Amber still had not told her parents about any of this, managing to keep it a secret from them for the last four months. Easter fell on Sunday, March 26. I was going to pick her up at her parents' house in Merced that night, meet them, and then drive back to school with her. Amber has five sisters, and Merced was a small farming community in central California. I felt like the city slicker traveling salesman passing through town to ruin the farmer's daughter. "Hi. I'm here to take your daughter away to jail now, sir."

While I was in town, Brooke, Amber, and I visited the Merced Zoo. It was a lonely, depressing place, with the few animals locked in cages. I didn't realize how much I'd have in common with them in a few days.

Chapter 20: Here Today Gone Tomorrow

Sentencing Day Eve. My parents had arrived in Chico; my brother, David, had come up with them. They all checked into the nicest hotel in town. I went to meet them for dinner. Amber stayed home to study for a test she had the next afternoon after we got sentenced. I suppose it would have been awkward, to say the very least, for her to meet my parents for the very first time under these circumstances.

Our dinner was awkward regardless. We all tried to make the best of it. I felt so horrible for putting my family through this ordeal, and vowed in a solemn toast that one day I would make them proud of me. My mother was mostly quiet and worried. My dad expounded on the importance of learning a life lesson from this experience. David joked about my choice of food for my last meal.

After dinner, my brother and I walked back to Amber's place through the streets of Chico. It was such a fun and seemingly inno-cent college town. Although it was only a Tuesday, people were already gearing up for the weekend. I wondered what I'd be doing this weekend.

When David met Amber for the first time, he tried to comfort her with some jail-type gallows humor. It worked a little, but she was extremely stressed. Afterward, he went back to the hotel, so it was just us now. Judgment Day was looming, and all the things we could've possibly said to each other had already been said. We were talked out. Amber made more half-hearted passes at studying. I made a half-hearted pass at her.

Chapter 21:

"I Fought the Law" and the Law Won

Judgment Day. If it sounds worse than it was, that's because it was. All the worries, the preparation, the money, and the anxiety could have been used on more worthy causes. My parents had been through the wringer. It was here that I would finally introduce them to Amber. She still had not told her parents, so they weren't there. Waiting for our ride, we said goodbye to our dogs, and told them we'd see 'em soon.

At 8:00 a.m. sharp, we heard the sound of gravel crunching in Amber's driveway. Looking out, we saw my parents in the front seats of their dark-gray Cadillac. It looked like a hearse—and to be fair, it did seem as though we were off to a funeral. We emerged dressed in our best courtroom attire and got into the American luxury car's king-sized, bed-like back seat, joining my always-wisecracking brother.

Amber had brought one of her schoolbooks, and asked my parents if they would mind if she studied for her upcoming test later that day. This both shocked and amused David. I was used to her taking every opportunity to sneak in a quick study session, but my parents hadn't seen much of that behavior in their own children. Although they'd had had built-in desks installed in our childhood bedrooms, these had rarely been used, except maybe to roll joints.

David and I stole glances at one another while Amber studied between us. Her test was for her psychology class. I was betting she could write an interesting term paper about this experience. I looked out the window as the single-car funeral procession motored on.

Our lawyers had expected that Amber's punishment would allow her to continue on with her work and school obligations. I had no idea what was in store for me. I was hoping for something like that, but feared something far more onerous. We tried to keep the mood light during the thirty-mile drive to the Butte County Superior Courthouse, (You can look up the review of the courthouse on Yelp. Yikes.) but I wished while Amber prayed that this would be the day we would be able to start putting this entire ordeal behind us.

Outside, it was glorious. The only cloud in the sky was hanging over our attorneys' faces as we arrived at the county complex. After we'd all gathered solemnly in the parking lot, my dad walked me up onto a little overlook for a last pep talk. We saw guys milling about in the county jail yard below us. I had never really seen convicted prisoners actually imprisoned. After a few moments, I looked away at the mountains. I was visualizing myself up there on one of them.

Brooke arrived, far more unsettled than Amber. Then came smug-faced Gustine, along with Amber's sad-faced parole officer. We had all prepped for a heavyweight title fight. Now it was time to step into the ring and face the judge.

Although the year was 1978 and the courthouse was brand spanking new, all the judges had been born near the turn of the century. Their judicial opinions ranged from ultra-conservative to positively medieval. This county sat distinctly outside the nationwide obsession with disco and frivolity. Everyone here seemed uptight. There was, however, one fairly comfortable attendee: little Arnie Gustine, barely concealing a crooked little smile with those rotted little rat teeth. His weaselly face could hardly contain his glee.

My father held a piece of paper that he nervously rolled into a tube, then pressed against his chin. My mother sat motionless. David looked confident. I was spaced out. Amber sat next to me with her head cast downward, buried in her psychology book, studying furiously for the test that she planned to take later.

The judge entered, and we all rose. My weight fell from my stomach to my feet. My entire mass was anchored in my toes. The rest of my body felt empty, untethered, and floating—one of those obnoxious plastic blow-up creatures with flailing arms but nothing inside, designed to attract attention as you drove past a local merchant.

The judge and the court clerk shuffled papers and cleared their throats. After a few long and very uncomfortable minutes, it was time for the reading of Amber's sentence.

"Miss Amber Jenson?"

She rose and weakly walked to face the judge. Attorney Kunkle, just as weakly, stood by her side.

"You have been found guilty of possession of and with the intent to distribute one hundred tablets of amphetamines."

These pills had less caffeine in them than a latte you would be able to buy in more than thirty-five thousand Starbucks locations forty years later.

The judge droned on. "I am very confused with what to do with you."

My ears perked up. That sounded promising . . . maybe just the middle of a fatherly lecture before he let her off with a stern warning. I was experienced in hearing those.

He continued. "To help ensure you will never make another decision like this one in the future, I have decided to send you to the women's state prison in Chowchilla, California, for a ninety-day observation for further evaluation."

I involuntarily screamed out, "*No!* Oh no! Please!" and then collapsed awkwardly onto my brother's chest. I couldn't believe these people had sent a first-time offender to state prison for selling caffeinated pills.

Amber was frozen. No emotion . . . at least outwardly and from the back. My beautiful princess turned to stone by the wicked judge. Kunkle tried to interject (the first time I heard his voice in court), but he was useless and helpless. Gustine snorted like a pig at its trough. Amber's PO stood up, brushing unhappily past us and out the front door of the courtroom, his recommendations ignored. Moments later, Amber too was led out through another door by two burly bailiffs. Watching in a haze, I heard my name being called.

"Richard Bruce Beren? Is he in the courtroom?"

Well, physically, yes. But his soul had left his body. Gustine, energized, leapt out of his seat and held open the little kiddy half gate that led me before the judge. I lurched out of my seat and the protective wrap of my brother's arms, weaving my way like a staggering drunk up to the now-vacant sentencing spot next to our attorney. The judge looked me up and down with little emotion; then he read aloud my various charges and offenses.

The sale of cocaine had been dropped—the actual percentage of cocaine had been too infinitesimal for even this draconian courtroom to pursue. Here I was, standing before the court, charged with the same crimes as Amber had been before me. What could I possibly expect the outcome for me to be? To be let free while she went to jail would have been a travesty. It would've even been worse than the one being perpetrated right now. I could not have lived with that consequence. My guilt would have overridden any technical innocence.

The judge began to utter words again, but they made no cognitive connection to my brain. My ability to assimilate information had evaporated. Was I in a courtroom in Afghanistan where they were speaking Pashto? Finally, I heard our attorney mumble some sort of acquiescence in English. It seemed I too had been sentenced to serve the ninety-day observation period, but at the men's state prison in Vacaville, California. Upon its completion and the ensuing evaluation from the Vacaville Prison psychologist, the judge promised to follow whatever recommendations might be meted out.

I was being escorted into custody when I heard a voice speak from the back of the courtroom. "Your honor?" the voice began. "Excuse me, your honor."

All the activity in the courtroom ceased. The disembodied voice was gaining strength and getting closer to me. The judge focused his attention on an eloquent gentleman. The man spoke of the needless waste and excessive danger of sending these two kids to state prison. He was suggesting a possible alternate solution—one that surely called for punishment, but that might with all due respect, be more commensurate with the crime. He begged the judge to reconsider.

My hopes lifted for this brief moment, but my heart was heavy at seeing and hearing this speaker—my father—have to plead for leniency for his very guilty son.

The judge listened politely and expressed appreciation for my dad's viewpoints. He also noted his heartfelt concerns. But, after careful consideration, he still believed his decision was for the best. Again. And more importantly, the judge did stress that he promised to abide by whatever recommendations the state prison evaluators' reports concluded.

Next to me, Gustine clenched his fist as if he had just made a game-winning three-point shot. I wished he were having a game-ending heart attack. I had risen expectantly to the top of a mighty wave, only to be forcefully crushed back down and ripped bloody on the jagged, sharp coral reef floor of the ocean. This was something I had become very familiar with these past few months.

Then I, too, was led away through the same doors as Amber. You've seen people led away from the courtroom on TV. Here's where they go. It's an empty little anteroom—although in this one, I saw a crumpled figure crouched in the corner, heaving and sobbing. I tried to rush to Amber to comfort her, but I was being restrained by several deputies. Helplessness now became my constant companion. My value as a man amounted to zero. Soon, it would sink even lower.

I stood there not six feet away, watching her cry. No one was allowed to enter this room except for convicted prisoners and their guards. I was concentrating so hard on Amber that I became incapable of seeing or hearing anyone or anything else. Suddenly, I felt arms around me and a soothing voice in my ear. Was I *already* becoming an inmate's love bitch?

Thank God, no. It was my father. Somehow, he had managed to have the judge allow him into this super-restricted area. My dad hugged me. Soon Amber was allowed to join us. My father was crying and actually apologizing to me! I had obviously been wrong when I believed that I couldn't have felt worse. I swore to my dad that I'd be strong and one day I'd make him cry for me out of pride. I apologized again and again for having put him through all this. I felt even worse for Amber. She did not have a loving and supportive father there for her. On one hand, her dad didn't have to suffer the pain that my father was suffering. On the other, she was alone. I don't know which I would have preferred. Yeah, I did.

Moments later, the guards separated us, leading Amber and me out one door and further into the jail while escorting my father out a different door and into freedom. We were ushered into a waiting police cruiser. The car was parked inside an enclosed cage. When we were safely ensconced inside the vehicle and the appropriate signal had been conveyed, the metal gate buzzed and began to roll open, allowing us to proceed. We were in the back seat of the police cruiser, handcuffed to one another and completely encapsulated behind strong wire mesh.

Amber's mood ranged from disbelief to despair. I knew this because those feelings pretty much mimicked my own. Add in shock. It was all of 10:00 a.m., for Christ's sake. It was hard to imagine that we weren't leaving with my family. It became clearer, and clearly more difficult, as the police car rounded the corner of the parking lot and I could see them standing there. They wore stunned expressions as we waved, our wrists handcuffed together. Aha! The notorious Chico State Juniors Drug Cartel had finally been brought to justice! Thousands, if not millions, of families in the greater Butte County area could rest easier tonight knowing that at least one hundred uppers had been taken off their streets.

Next to me, Amber began to babble, asking many questions, none of which I had the answers for. Who knew where we were going and what was in store for us? This was before Google. We couldn't have looked such a thing up. Then, Amber would giggle and shake her head as if to wake up from this bad dream. I could only see her long hair hanging down, stuck to her face from the tears that had streamed down it. She was a mess. More guilt for me—yay. My stupidity had hurt those that I held so dear to me. I felt an inner rage, but I tried to retain an outer placidity.

"I don't even have any money," she realized, addressed to no one in particular. She had only the clothes on her back—she had been able to hand off her ever-present textbook to Brooke.

I contorted my body and managed to extract twenty dollars from my front pocket. My high-waisted jeans and my highest-ever weight made that task nearly impossible. "No more of passing that shit," one deputy warned us sternly.

We arrived two minutes later at a large outside structure. It was the automobile intake area of the Butte County Jail. Immediately in front of us stood a twelve-foot-high cyclone fence topped by three feet of barbed wire. With a loud, electric buzz, the gate began to slowly slide open, which allowed the cruiser to drive forward into a space just large enough for the car to fit. Once the engine was turned off, the buzz again reverberated throughout the car, the gate reversing its path until it clanged securely shut. Here we sat, still handcuffed, inside a wire-mesh-enclosed basket in the back seat of a police cruiser, which was itself completely surrounded by a twelve-foot-high cyclone fence topped by three feet of barbed wire. A cage inside a car inside a cage. And handcuffed.

Next, we were shuttled into another area, then sequestered until the perimeter was locked and secured. We were then led out of the car and herded into yet another room. The guards were armed with electric prods and batons, ensuring that our paths did not deviate. Those thirty or so seconds were designed to squeeze the last vestiges of freedom from anybody's soul. Like cattle.

We repeated this procedure three more times, escorted from one secured cubicle on to another locked sector. It was as if we had arrived in our ship from outer space at the docking area, which would then be air-sealed before the inner door to the next chamber could open.

Finally, we arrived at the prisoners' intake area. We were motioned toward the "booking cage." I knew this because there was a stenciled sign above it that clearly read "Booking Cage." It wasn't like you needed directions—it was the only place to go—but if we did, there were fifteen traffic cops five feet in front of us. The booking cage was little more than another cyclone-fenced-in cage. Think of it as the front desk of a nice hotel, except that it isn't nice and there are no smiling concierges.

We stood side by side, still handcuffed, apparently huge flight risks. They collected our "valuables," which amounted to next to nothing—I had given Amber my only money. Then we were uncuffed and handed county-issued bedrolls, supple and comfortable as a stack of two-by-fours. They allowed Amber to change into her jail uniform behind a burlap curtain; it was a sack, all her one-hundred-pound frame lost in it. Paperwork was sorted swiftly, and Amber's name was called.

There wasn't a lot more to say, and a lot of guys standing between us had I tried. But there was still everything I *wanted* to say. I wanted to tell her that everything would be okay, but I didn't think that would have really assured her. I tried to say something, but I just didn't have any words. They had been vacuumed out of me.

Amber took four steps to the steel door to begin her sentence. She turned, and we locked eyes. Hers were filled with tears.

"Goodbye, Rick. Please take care."

And with that, I watched her walk down a long concrete hallway, led by her prison matron, until the heavy door slammed shut.

"You too, hon. Oh God, you too."

I crumpled onto a wooden bench like I would've if Joe Frazier had hit me below the belt with one of those violent uppercuts intended for Muhammad Ali's jaw. I sat there sucking in deep breaths, the wind knocked out of me. Soon my lungs had filled back up with cigarette smoke. An inmate had begun to feed me cigarettes. Was he my friend?

He was, as I would learn later, a snitch, but they called him a "trusty." That was why he was up here with the guards. It was for his protection. Someone was out to hurt him in some fashion—and me, it might turn out, if I were around him too long. I was gonna need a travel guide for this place.

Right then, my lungs were hurting from the unfiltered Camel cigarettes I was chain-smoking. I may have smoked a half dozen already. It was 11:30 a.m., I was dizzy, and I had a massive headache. I really hadn't ever been much of a smoker. I sat there trying to look mean, but the scowl on my face was mostly from fear, confusion, and sadness. I sat in this part of the facility for an hour, but it felt like I had completed half of my ninety days. Thoughts whizzed and bounced around my head like pachinko balls.

A door opened and a guard told me to go into another room, which was a space twelve feet long and three feet wide. Inside were four metal stools cemented to the ground, spaced evenly apart. Each stool had a phone in front of it on a steel ledge. In front of all the stools and phones was an unbreakable, three-inch-thick glass window. This I recognized from movies as the visitors' room. On the other side, I saw the exact same setup. Prisoners and visitors were separated only by this three-inch glass. The rooms were empty.

Just then, to my amazement, four delighted faces streamed into the empty area on the visitors' side. They all sported huge grins. When my parents, my brother, and Brooke appeared in front of me, I immediately thought to myself, hopefully, that maybe this had all been an elaborate joke. They all looked so cheerful. Was the case being dropped? Had my father come up and hit a grand slam with two outs in the bottom of the ninth to win the game? Yes, yes! Pick up the phone! Please tell me the good news! Hurry!

My dad took the telephone, attached by a two-foot-long stainless-steel cord, and held it up to his mouth. "Hi, Ricky-poo!"

I didn't think many of the conversations in this room had begun with someone calling the prisoner "Ricky-poo," but he had always called me that when I was young and he was happy with me. I guessed that now he would call me that when I was a stupid, ass-fuck loser too.

I ran to the similar setup on my side and picked up the phone. "Hi, Dad. What's going on?!"

An inane question—I was locked away in a county jail speaking to him through a ridiculous device which amounted to little more than a concoction of two Campbell's soup cans connected by a string, plaintively staring at him some three feet away, separated by (I imagined) super-thick bulletproof glass. What was going on was that I was horrified to have put these people in this room. I belonged locked up, just for the pain I had caused my parents. Throw away the key.

No. The sentence had not been tossed. This was not an elaborate prank. The people I loved were trying their hardest to give me a boost. They were rallying to appear strong for me. Unfortunately, I could see through the plastered-on smiles into the dullness of their eyes.

"The lieutenant gave us special permission to talk to you. Isn't that nice?"

My father was obviously playing to the guards, who were listening to our conversation.

"Yeah, real sweet," I mumbled. I was not in a very gracious frame of mind. "I'm sorry, Dad," I said as I watched even more life drain from his eyes. I hadn't even thought that was possible. They were usually blue. Now they were pale gray.

"I know that. Just be good and it will be over soon. It could be as soon as forty-five days if they process you quickly down there!"

Down there. Jesus. It sounded so menacing.

"So now it's up to you," he continued. "No more Gustine."

He and I both visibly winced at the mention of the name. He had become our personal Voldemort before there even was such a character. Maybe J. K. Rowling based him on Arnold Gustine.

"I love you, Dad." I wished so much to be able to hug him, but I had to be content communicating it via a greasy, corded steel wire.

"I love you, my son," he replied, shakily handing the phone to my mother.

She took his place at the other end of the cord and began to talk to me as if I were heading off to summer camp—a Jewish one at that. "Now, brush your teeth, and you can write often—oh!" I waited for a pearl of wisdom. "And make sure you have clean underwear," she added rather awkwardly. It was all rather awkward.

Then I asked, "How is Amber doing?"

There was a pregnant pause. They all rushed to fill the silence with overly exuberant and somewhat unbelievable replies of "She's *great*!" and "Not to worry" and "Keep it together," reverberating thinly throughout the room. How's that song go? *Smiling faces, sometimes . . . they don't tell the truth.*

The visit was slowly going down the drain. Their intention of cheering me up seemed to be in vain. David slipped into the spot on the other side of the phone. We were sitting directly across from one another like we had for so many years at the family dinner table. The Gaza Strip, you might've said, had you been there for dinner.

I felt the concrete at my knees separating us. "I wish I had this setup all those years ago at dinner when you were kicking me under the table," I managed.

"You want to trade places?" he offered.

I chuckled. He always could make me laugh, even while torturing me.

"I knew I could get you," he stated proudly.

"Yeah," I glumly agreed.

"You loser. Nobody goes to jail for this. I can't believe it."

"*You* can't?" I was in total shock. This place was like some throwback town in the Deep South in the 1950s. I managed, "I really fucked up, didn't I?"

"Yeah. Just keep your back to the wall and sit down a lot."

"Yeah, I'll bend at the knees when I pick stuff up off the floor."

I asked again about Amber, and David's demeanor shifted, though he quickly recovered. "She's fine. She's right next to you. She says not to worry about her." I could see the strained look on his face. It did not make me not worry about her.

David had always been an extremely mean bully. He had also been a big high-school baseball star with a powerful throwing arm and pinpoint accuracy. He could chuck a rock or a ball from a hundred feet away, making sure it curved in perfectly, landing painfully at my arm or my back—or head, if he so desired. I was seeing another side of his personality now. He was still a bully and an asshole when we were growing up, but he visited me a lot and wrote often during my time in jail.

Then Brooke picked up the phone. She had been talking to Amber some six feet away on my immediate right, but out of my sight due to a wall that separated the male and female prisoners. Brooke's mascara was running down her face from the tears, but . . . she tried to squeeze out a smile.

"Hi, Rick. What are you doing?"

"Oh gee. Nothing in particular, Brooke. I just thought I'd get my stupid ass locked up in this shithole for the next few months. You?"

I would also receive many letters from Brooke. Amber and I were not allowed to communicate with one another prison to prison at that time, so Brooke would be liaison for letters between the two of us, including my letter with the one she was sending to Amber. I addressed those letters to "Amberly"—a verifiable criminal mastermind, you could say. I only obtained permission to write to Amber directly after a couple of months.

"Be strong, Rick," Brooke said as our eyes locked. Then she looked around to see if anyone was listening and leaned in. She whispered, "Your brother is a fox."

I guess priorities were priorities. I claimed that I was the better-looking brother.

"Well, don't try to be Mr. Universe in there," she advised. It was true—I shouldn't flaunt my recently professed good looks in state prison. We both heard steel doors clang closed behind me. God only knew what was in store for me back there.

Then, casually, she said, "Hey! Do you want to talk to Amber?"

My eyes lit up. "What? How?"

She told me to move to the stool on my side that was closest to the wall and pick up the phone. Then she went over to Amber's side and instructed her to do the same. The prisoners' side of the room was divided by a thick wall separating men from women, but on the visitors' side, you could pass freely between both areas. I guess this would make it convenient for those lucky kids whose parents happened to get locked up at the same time. She picked up the two receivers on the visitors' side that corresponded with ours and twisted the talking part of each phone next to the listening part. This is how we used to conference call. We could sort of hear each other through the metallic lines.

"Hey! I see you in the reflection."

The world's very first (and worst) FaceTime. Dim, but I cherished that image for a long time.

"Can you believe this?" I said to her.

"Yeah. Lucky I met you that night, mister." Bravado. All false.

At that moment, a screeching of shrill whistles followed by a loud buzzer careened off the walls of the small visitors' chambers. In burst one of the strongest-looking women I had ever seen in my life. I mean, her eyebrows had biceps. She screamed out orders, and assuredly escorted our visitors out of the room. Their fake smiles were rapidly wiped off their faces.

"Get those convicts off the damn phones!" shrieked the woman, who I would later learn was named Helen.

"'Convicts'?" My new moniker landed with a resounding thud.

I was bum-rushed out, taken down a dark corridor, and deposited in front of a young, forlorn-looking nurse. She had a severe case of acne and bottle-thick glasses. We shared a look, and I wondered what in the hell had brought us together today in this room. The reason would soon become clear.

"Please leave us, Rebecca," the biggest of the squad platoon kindly asked the nurse. He didn't have to ask her twice.

"All right, Fuck-Dick. You listen good now."

My listening skills were compromised by an immediate forearm shiver to my jaw. I wasn't about to correct his grammar either—prone on the filthy floor, I stared up at three guards who loomed over me as they eagerly searched for vulnerable spots to land more hurtful blows. Their ages ranged from just a few years older than me to one who looked to be about my father's age. He gave a neat kick to what would've been my groin if I hadn't deftly defended myself (my quick reflexes sharply honed thanks to multiple battles with my brother), thereby saving my future ability to sire children—though my near future of having sex looked dubious if this kept up. They only knocked me around for a minute or so, but you'd be surprised how many successful hits six arms, six legs, and three sticks can accomplish in such a relatively short amount of time.

"Don't ever fuck up again with bullshit like that phone call you just pulled!"

One more carefully crafted steel-toed boot to the ribcage (it's still sore when I breathe in deeply forty years later), and just like that, again with no impromptu grammar lesson, it was over. They left me there in a heap.

Jesse, the trusty, entered, helped me to my feet, and led me to a large laundry bin (the kind prisoners use to escape), telling me to pick out my "new clothes." I chose a well-worn pair of jeans (they may have been Levi's—from the Gold Rush era), size thirty-eight waist. I was actually about a thirty waist, but this was the closest size available. I was also outfitted with a medium-sized blue work shirt. It still resonated with the odious body stench of its previous inhabitant. My first jailhouse uniform. I was now officially "Jailhouse Rick."

I put my courtroom clothes in a bag and handed them over to Jesse, where they would be ostensibly waiting for me upon my release. Nice threads, I thought, certain I would never see that brushed suede jacket with the faux fur collar again. A new guard appeared (*How many do they have in this joint?!*), saw that the fitting session had been completed (no three-sided mirrors to check out how your ass looked), and motioned me further into my new jail home. I limped as slowly as possible—no, not because my ribs were killing me (and they were) but because I was searching every nook and cranny for any sight of Amber. Plus, I was carrying my bedroll with one hurting arm and holding up the enormous jeans that kept falling off my very sore body with my other hand.

We walked past two cells that housed twelve men, each sitting on cots. I had never been so close to such a collection of miserable- and angry-looking guys in my life. I was thankful to be protected from them by these thick bars and the officer. Then it dawned on me. I was being brought to live amongst and become one of these men.

We stopped at a heavy iron gate. We had reached the murkiest area. The door slid open. Eleven souls were sitting in front of me on the floor; their outstretched legs blocked my entrance. Twenty-two eyes stared vacantly up at me like coal miners who had been stuck in a cave for days. There was no indication that anyone was going to move. I shifted my bedroll to assure a firm grip; I did not want it or anything of mine to accidentally fall onto someone and cause a problem. I especially did not want my very loose pants to drop to my ankles. I held onto both tightly and moved forward with trepidation. With each step, a pair of legs would slowly and begrudgingly contract out of my way. I really had no plan as to where I was headed. I suppose I was looking for an empty cot to place my thin mattress on. Once I found a rack that was empty, I unfolded my gear and sat down on my new home. I rubbed my eyes with my palms and furiously massaged my scalp, a behavior I'd find myself repeating several hundred times that day.

A full minute of my sentence had now elapsed. I had a lot of time ahead of me. I looked around, my eyes beginning to focus on my bleak surroundings. No windows. Completely barred in. No escape. I know the sun must've been shining somewhere. It still couldn't have been much past noon. I sat on my bunk, pulled my legs up, and curled myself into a tight ball. I was trying to look as much like a hardened criminal as I possibly could. I wondered if that was the way. I had no template for how to be; no guidelines, no instruction manual. Did I act tough and encourage someone to challenge me? Or should I act like a harmless idiot, which I truly was? I did not know how to read jail social norms. I was on the spectrum here. I had prison autism. On pure instinct, I managed to quickly calculate that it was better to be quiet and observe. I needed to learn how to behave properly in order to survive. I was exhausted, but extremely wired and too petrified to close my eyes—unfortunate, as it was pure agony to even blink due to the searing pain in my head. My ribs didn't feel great either.

People began shuffling about. Outside this cell was the hallway I had just been led through. Downtrodden men were grumbling and murmuring. This hallway was closer to the outer world, but still devoid of natural lighting or windows. As my eyes adjusted to the darkest corner of the twelve-man cell, I saw there was a steel cot soldered to the wall next to me, just like mine and all the other eleven cots in this bunker. Each cot was inches apart, meaning that when I slept, my head would be inches from another man's feet or head.

My new neighbor was sitting on his cot. He was stripped naked to the waist and completely covered in tattoos. A stream of blood dripped between his piercing black eyes. I tried not to stare or react in any outward fashion, but we were less than two feet apart. I may have raised my eyebrows slightly, like Mr. Spock might have. No words were exchanged between us. We just sat there as if nothing had just happened to me. Which would hopefully be the case. It was as if this went on every day—which, come to think of it, it did.

I became aware of activity down the hallway: chains and heavily barred doors opening. My fellow inmates exited toward the noises and rumbled down the hall. Was the prison being overrun? *Who do I side with? Will I be an escapee on my first day? Will I be a hostage?*

"Lunch!" someone bellowed from afar.

Food was about the last thing on my mind. I had expected this day to be resolved in a completely different way. Amber and I should've been at a reserved yet relieved lunch with my parents, then off to attend our classes, our homes, our dogs. *Our dogs!* Who was going to take care of our dogs? I would worry about Walker more than anything or anyone else. Because we hadn't expected this outcome, we hadn't settled any of our day-to-day things. One minute, we had cars, clothes, and $1 put down toward the $2.99 price for the new Stones album (*Some Girls*, coming out the next month at Tower Records in Chico). The next, we were stripped and issued Butte County Jail button-down shirts and jeans. I never picked up that record.

The cell emptied, but I was not in the mood for food or socializing. I stayed and tried to think of anything I could besides the headache that was still dominating inside my skull. I was nauseous. I had to throw up, but there was nothing in my stomach, so I had the dry heaves.

Normally I might've hoped to close my eyes and tune out the sound and the light, maybe grab a few aspirin from the medicine cabinet. But this was far from normal, at least the normal I was used to. I could not control the sounds or the light. There was no fresh air or cold towel to wrap around my head. There was no medicine cabinet in the bathroom. In fact, there *was* no bathroom—just a bowl to squat on in the middle of the cell. Yes, if you had to take a shit, you had to do it right there while eleven other guys were within twenty feet of you, sitting, smoking, playing cards, jerking off (yep), or napping. Although in my case, I was blessed, as our communal toilet was a mere three feet from my cot. No wonder it was the only spot available. *Location, location, location.*

There was zero privacy. I had nothing but the clothes on my back and a load of new troubles on my mind. My thoughts always landed back at Amber. Think of experiencing this without sending (or receiving) four hundred texts and selfies. It's just you and yourself.

Shaking my heavy, hurting head, I could not believe how I had gone from looking for an apartment in Chico with my buddy to looking for bed space in the local county jail.

I looked down at my shoes. I was wearing Famolare "Get There" shoes. The irony was not lost on me.

My father was a pretty big deal in the shoe business. He used to have about twenty-five retail stores. "Get There," with the wavy soles, were the darlings of the industry at that time. I must have sold hundreds of pairs of them myself. My dad's stores had sold thousands. I also sold a ton (they almost weighed a ton) of Baretraps, and the delightfully light Sbiccas. Anyway, for some reason I, and only I, was allowed to continue wearing my classic Famolare shoes throughout my entire visit to the California prison system. I never saw anyone else wearing a pair. More miraculously, no one asked or bothered me about these newfangled-looking shoes. I suppose I could've been killed just for wearing them. Who knows what (or whom) they may have triggered? Maybe the other prisoners thought these weird-looking shoes were for a physical disability I had. Anything out of the ordinary could cause unwarranted and unwanted attention. If they only knew I would've readily given the shoes up in a second if anyone had bothered. I would've even waived my 10 percent commission (about $2.90).

I sat cross legged on my cot in my space. My world had been reduced to six feet by two feet. I felt like a little guppy in a fluorescent-lit aquarium with sharks all around me. The pressure was building inside my skull, like the temperature gauge on a steamship with the shrill whistle right before it explodes. You know when you go to the doctor and they have you circle a number from one to ten, with ten being the absolute worst pain? Well, this pain was an eleven. I was having a full-blown migraine.

I really hadn't looked around or engaged with anyone. I didn't know if I was supposed to shake hands or look someone in the eye like when you say hello. It was a foreign planet. *What's the protocol?* I figured it was best to just stay to myself, just observe. I was locked up with eleven other convicted felons of varying unknown degrees of criminal history, so I thought it best to avoid or defer any action of any kind.

Even though there was an abundance of police presence in here, none of them appeared to be jumping up and down, urgent to fulfill their sworn motto "to protect and to serve." I'd soon learn that hourly fistfights between inmates were basically ignored by the authorities. Blood or maybe a broken bone sticking out of a body part might've brought a response from the officer in charge, but who knew? There was no rush, either. There seemed to me to be plenty of time and space to get my ass kicked, so I kept my mouth shut. Have I mentioned that I'm about five feet seven inches and at that time weighed 140 pounds soaking wet? I had to use my brains in an altercation (and look where that had gotten me thus far), as brawn was not gonna be an option.

It was such a strange environment. Here you had a group of individuals who were forcibly directed and corralled at all times. On the other hand, you had a smaller (though armed) faction who were bound to keep these people sequestered to serve their allotted sentence. The closest I could correlate this to anything I had experienced was being forced to attend Hebrew school.

Turns out the guy next to me was named Bob. Bob was only a couple years older than I; however, it was obvious the years had been harder on him. He had been here several times, currently for armed assault and a host of other misdeeds. He was in a white nationalist biker gang, and was in the process of inking a gang insignia tattoo in between his eyes. His waist-length black hair was knotted in a ponytail at the top of his head. Bob was the first guy in jail to whom I told the story of how I came be sitting next to him.

I always got many different responses from my fellow prisoners when I shared my tale. Some would shake their heads or let out a moan or low whistle at the relatively minor offense that had gotten me imprisoned, especially relative to the crimes that had gotten them incarcerated. Some would look at me suspiciously and think I had to be an undercover narc, but my story was so ludicrous that the thought would soon be dismissed. Bob was kind of stunned, but not surprised by the sentence for the paltry quantity of drugs that had landed me here; he understood the local legal system and wearily said that I had just been "in the wrong place at the wrong time." That pretty well summed it up. Jailhouse logic—it cuts right to the chase. He sympathized to a degree. Hell, everyone had a lot of their own shit in here, and mine was minor league. Fact is, nobody really gave a fuck, but he really thought it was harsh that my girlfriend got busted too.

Bob was also on his way to Vacaville. He had been sentenced to fourteen years. He was currently busy wrapping and loading marijuana into bubble-gum-sized plastic balls and putting them up his ass to transport for market at Vacaville. Very industrious. Despite myself, I took a liking to my new compatriot. Brothers-in-arms drugs salesmen. He had a unique delivery system and was laser-beam focused on pleasing his clientele. I watched him with a combination of revulsion and fascination.

Bob was my new best friend. He proved this by telling me everything about himself (I was already intimate with one thing about him). Bob also held another allure for me (not that his bottomless-ass capacity wasn't already enough): he had cartons of cigarettes. Better yet, he had cartons of Marlboro Reds. "Come to Where the Flavor Is." I wonder what the flavor of the pot coming from Bob's ass would taste like.

I was in a different kind of Marlboro Country now. The smokes surrounded his cot like a fortress. To me, they looked like bricks of gold—they were my cigarette of choice, and I really needed to smoke. I hadn't come prepared, I suppose. Who knew? Plus, I gave Amber my only twenty bucks, so I couldn't buy any. Bob figured I was good for it when I said I'd get some money. Surprisingly, here was the second inmate to feed me cigarette after cigarette.

A pack of cigarettes cost about thirty-five cents then. I smoked a cigarette every ten to fifteen minutes for a while. Sometimes I'd light my new cigarette off the burning stub of the previous one. Bob called this maneuver "butt fucking." I hoped he didn't have any other butt-fucking maneuvers in mind. I figured the most I could rack up was maybe a five-dollar debt. What could possibly go wrong—me owing five bucks to an oft-convicted, drug-dealing, possibly sociopathic felon, who . . . built like the bricks that housed us, able to carve himself without a sound where I would have cried from a splinter like the baby I was . . . and whom I was currently locked up with?

Bob was very prepared. I listened as if he were Yoda. I was admittedly pretty surprised about the kinds of crimes people were out there plotting and perpetrating. It was their verifiable job—a career, if you will. It takes a lot of time, dedication, and devotion to concoct these atrocities. I learned that prison time was "just collateral damage. The price of doing business." It didn't seem to faze, bother, or scare anyone in here, or so they all swore. At the doorstep of Bob's house (actually the foot of his cot), I heard the first of many criminal adventures that had eventually landed him in front of me. I was chain-smoking and nodding my head appropriately in what I hoped were the right places. The next few hours he would spend musing about how to plan to perfect the crime to not get caught the next time. Often the solution would be to eliminate the witnesses. I would try to maintain neutrality at this portion of the conversation, nodding slightly in response and hoping my gulp was inaudible, but I must admit, I was extremely fucking freaked out. I mean, he was talking murder here. Was I now complicit? Would I now be on the to-be-murdered list? Inside my frazzled brain rattled loudly, *Why not just* not *do the crime?* I'd say it to myself, because it seemed to make so much more sense to me. *But didn't you also commit a crime?* I'd also say to myself. Me and myself would have a lot of conversations like this one. Bob had calculated that his fourteen years would be reduced with good time served to about four or five years.

Everyone was talking about the Jarvis-Gann initiative, known as Proposition 13, currently slated to appear on the upcoming California ballot in a couple months. It was to be a major tax over-haul. Funny how it affected people from all walks of life differently. I think my parents and their friends were much more interested in paying less property tax on their magnificent homes. Some of those grand mansions with three bridge views of the entire San Francisco Bay were fetching almost six figures. The prison population (inmates *and* guards), however, was deeply interested in how this would affect the budgets of the state's penal institutions. Less money for guarding the prisoners . . . less prison time for the prisoners. California has a huge prison industry. There is a lot of money to be made locking people in jail—especially people of color, but on that day a scared, rich, spoiled little white Jewish boy.

I heard another loud commotion down the hall—rustling, shuf-fling, clamoring, jostling. I got up and looked out. All the doors were automatically sliding open. Were we being released? Olly olly oxen free! Oh joy! I excitedly walked toward the doors, ready to rejoin my friends, my family, my dog, and Amber. Instead, through those doors I had entered what already felt like a lifetime ago came clomping a bedraggled trail of guys, all dressed in various forms of Butte County Jail–themed threads. This grungy group filed past me with barely a nod or a grunt. They were coming back from lunch. Next loomed five hours of sitting around in a semi-darkened cave reminiscent of the medieval dungeons recently unearthed underneath the Louvre. There was nothing to do except watch various guys while they took loud, loose, vile-smelling bowel movements mere inches in front of me until dinner.

So I leaned back into my cot. And I sat. And I smoked. Then Bob performed another miracle: he gave me a paperback book! I hadn't even thought of that. I loved to read. It was a cheesy, B-level Matt Helm detective series book. You might remember the movies starring Dean Martin. I hadn't ever heard of them. I hungrily grabbed it, and with my eyes perpetually adjusting to the omnipresent gloom, I tore into the adventure. This would be the first of hundreds of books I would read while serving my time. I figured if I focused my mind in a book, I could as well be sitting in a beach chair on the French Riviera, reading the same story. The trick was to not look up from the pages. Bob napped. I read. Men shit.

The imaginary clock ticked so slowly. You think watching the clock tick to three on the last day of school before summer vacation when you're in second grade is slow? That's child's play in comparison. I sensed another movement. The doors down the hall shuddered and rumbled open. Could it be dinner already? This time I was curious—not hungry, but wondering where I actually was and if I would be able to see Amber where dinner was being served. "Table for two, please, sir?"

I made my way past the heavy, iron-barred door and down the hall. Around the corner, I caught a glimpse of the outdoors! Trees! Sky and probably fresh air! My head swiveled back and forth for any sight of Amber. Nothing. We were deposited into a room with five round tables. On top of them were small paper sacks, evenly spread out. Our release documents?

I reached into my sack to discover it contained only a bologna sandwich, a small apple, and a warm carton of milk. I was crushed. I had really expected this ordeal to mystically come to an end, that everyone would break out laughing at the ridiculousness.

I sat in silence, managed a sideways glimpse around the room, and caught quick glances of my roomies in a bit better lighting now. This could not be mistaken for an open casting call for leading soap opera star roles. I suppose I wasn't ready to compete with Ted Danson in those early 1980s Aramis cologne commercials either. After fifteen or so minutes, the guys began to wrap up their meals. Never wanting to waste food (a lesson drilled into me by my beloved Nana), I pocketed my apple and milk. I did manage to throw away the slice of meat tucked between two dry pieces of Wonder Bread—it was supposed to be bologna, but the sides were tinged green, and I didn't think it was because it was an olive and pimento loaf.

I brought the apple and milk back for Bob and casually offered my food to him. He took them, then slowly put his head down. I didn't know if he was going to lift his head up and threaten to kill me or what. When he did bring his eyes up to mine, they were filled with tears.

He said, "Nobody has ever done anything like that for me in my life."

The rest of the night, I listened to Bob quietly tell me his life story. Hell, I didn't have anywhere else to be. It entailed abuse at a young age, a lot of neglect, and then an early foray into drugs and violence. He'd joined a motorcycle gang and dropped out of school by the age of fourteen, which was roughly the same time he had committed his first violent felony.

It was not lost on me that he'd had little opportunity, whereas I'd had nothing but. Yet here we sat side by side, the same roof over our heads. Bob was an interesting and intelligent guy. He shared many cigarettes with me, perhaps three packs. I had never in my life smoked more than half a pack of cigarettes in a day, but this really wasn't your typical day. I didn't even know if it was night or day. The light inside never varied.

I spoke a bit. When I did, it was mostly about Amber. Bob took it upon himself to help me to send her a message. I learned that in jail parlance, this is called a "kite." Somehow, some way (there was always a way in here), someone, for something in exchange (always), got a written note to someone in an area that the two (or more) people could not physically meet in. Amber and I were those two people. We filled all the criteria perfectly. It was very frowned upon. Naturally, I was all in.

Bob was a romantic. After listening to my story, with stunning and rapid expertise, he organized a cabal that agreed to pass along my message—a note that would have to go through thick walls and land in the women's area. I filled it with guilt and remorse and love and encouragement. It made me feel better to connect with Amber, even in some abstract fashion. The message delivered, I drifted off into a fitful first night's sleep.

I never considered that there could be ramifications. I guess this jail sentence hadn't changed me much yet.

Chapter 22:

Good Morning Good Morning

March 30, 1978. My first morning in jail.

Loud shouts and clanging. I opened my eyes. My vision was blurred. I found myself six inches from a cinder-block wall. I could've almost tasted (if there had been any saliva in my mouth) the black mold on it. *Oh, Lord. Please let this be one of those extremely realistic dreams. Let it be one of those where you've even dreamt that you are awake and it's awful, but then you actually order yourself to really awaken and it's just been an awful dream.*

Yeah. This isn't one of those. But let me hope for a moment. I'm home now, right? I'm in bed with Amber. This is all a crazy hallucination. The noise is the dogs barking. That's the commotion. My biggest concern is that I have a paper due in my English lit class tomorrow. That's okay. I always wait until it's almost too late. I closed my eyes again for as long as I could, still hoping that when I opened them, I wouldn't be in the place I had a sinking feeling I really was. Then I turned over and opened them.

Yuck. I witnessed an amalgamation of down-on-their-luck men rising and shuffling, about to face another empty day. What compelled these people? How could they have been in this place (or any other remotely like it) and continue on the path that led them back to such an environment?

My headache still felt like a chainsaw zigzagging through the top of my skull, slicing through my eyeballs, replete with the high-pitched whining sound of the shards of my brains being stuffed into a wood chipper. It was all consuming, perhaps the worst one I have ever had—and when I was ten, I was rushed to the hospital for a brain scan because of debilitating headaches. *Hey! We should've used "previous brain damage" as a defense strategy! Anything would've been better than what our fine counsel mounted. Only thing they successfully mounted was me.*

Watching the withered, weathered, mostly older men's bodies was depressing enough, but then an oily fume overtook my nostrils and made my eyes sting. I panned over to embrace the view of a seventy-five-year-old man, sitting not more than two feet from me and letting his puckered old asshole open up and punish that metal toilet bowl. The sound was that of a Caribbean steel drum player of squirts and lumps hitting the various sweet spots below. My meager appetite was about to be lost . . . forever. This had to be some sort of violation of human rights. I alone seemed to have the abject horror of the circumstance seared into my brain.

So now all five of my senses had been assaulted.

Touch: I had woken up to my face touching a wall coated in grime from the day my cell had first been inhabited, some three decades earlier. You didn't exactly have the maid coming in here twice a week (or between guests' visits) to clean. There was the added bonus of a nice accumulation of black mold growing on the wall inches from my face.

Smell: The oily gases that had escaped from my cellmates and wafted into my proximity were causing mouth-breathing.

Taste: The many packs of cigarettes I'd smoked in the past twenty hours—no open window—and stacks of butts crushed in the ashtray by my bunk, not to mention the dozen other smokers in this barely oxygenated environment, left my throat and mouth sore and my saliva basically liquid nicotine seeping down my throat.

Sight: My eyes had unfortunately adjusted, but my mind was still recoiling at the image projecting into them: a man my grandfather's age finishing up his bowel movement, a "gimme putt" away from my face.

Sound: The shits were schplooting out of his ass and careening into the metal toilet bowl in squirts and splashes.

I held a full house. Now I was gripped with a case of claustrophobia, not unlike when you are a teen and your mom says on a summer afternoon, "Why don't you go somewhere?" only for you to say, "There's nowhere to go." In this case *there was literally nowhere to go!* I first would have had to navigate past Grandpa Shitsville, and even then I was still in a locked forty-by-twenty-foot cage with eleven other guys.

Just then, my next move was made for me. The cellblock doors automatically slid open at the command of an unseen controller. Who could blame the operator for not walking down this hallway? (Or "hellway," as I saw it.) I was first in line in the cluster as the gates slowly opened, hightailing it down the hall for not-so-fresh fresh air.

Breakfast consisted of a sort of mealy oatmeal concoction. I imagine it wasn't much different than the concoction the old man had deposited into the toilet some thirty seconds before. Had that really just happened half a minute ago, in my life? I mustered a couple of bites and tried to squeeze some juice from the two dry orange slices. Coffee was passed around in a banged-up metal pitcher like an old cowboy campfire urn. Our coffee was see-through. Quite weak. Definitely not Peet's. I sat mute at my table. By then my escape fantasies had become muted.

A guy passed by and told me that my kite had successfully flown. Hooray! I'd succeeded in prison! I had Bob to thank for that. I looked up and noticed that he was also not in the room. I got up and looked around as far as the fifteen feet the eye could see. I was hoping for a glimpse of Amber. On my own, I was not a prison success story.

We were guided back to our large toilet bowl—I mean, cramped living quarters. I went to my house and saw that Bob's stuff was gone. Was it something I said? It couldn't have been my breath, even though I hadn't brushed my teeth, 'cause nothing could complete with Grampa Shitsalot back here. Bob had vanished. *What the fuck?*

Eventually, another veteran let me know that Bob had been transferred to a more secure area of the Butte County Jail before being transferred down to Vacaville—"the joint," the "big house," state prison. This was where they would induct each incoming California State prisoner and evaluate where his sentence would next be served most peacefully. I was scheduled to be sent to Vacaville and evaluated myself. I hoped they evaluated me the fuck out of there.

It was like applying to colleges in reverse. I was trying to get out of the system. Remember, the judge in Butte County had promised to abide by the forthcoming Vacaville reports. This was mainly to mollify Gustine and his expressed desire to lock me up for the rest of my twenties.

For now, I sat in my little spot. There was a flat, empty metal space where Bob's world had previously existed. He had kindly left me with Matt and a pack of cigarettes. Gulp. *What might that cost me?*

I immersed myself in my Matt Helm story. What would Matt have done? The headache had not ceased; I guessed no fresh air, coupled with my and others' constant smoking, zero food, and barely one cup of very weak coffee, was a great recipe for the colossal pounding migraine. Oh yeah, and an inordinate amount of fear and stress.

You would think putting together a bunch of guys with nothing to do would be boring. It was. But these were a host of ne'er-do-wells, and they were continually on the lookout for causing trouble. Guys were milling about. Not much conversation or interaction. Nobody really wanted to get in anyone's way, least of all me.

After breakfast, I was sitting on my bed when a full-blown fight to the death erupted on the floor inches from my face. One of the guys attempted to swing a sock loaded with a bar of soap in it (turns out, a pretty lethal weapon) into another guy's skull. (His only crime seemed to be that he was Native American.) Thankfully, it hit a steel girder first, and the soap imploded into dust inside the sock before it could do that to the other guy's brain. This was not a fight for intellectual superiority. I guess I had learned a thing or two—I knew if I expressed any interest in this battle, I would become someone's future target. Instead, I feigned disinterest.

Yeah. Things were tense. I kept my head down in my book, but even that behavior could cause a problem—if they think you're too smart, too *anything*, you stick out and draw someone's ire. It was an older man's *Lord of the Flies* world in here. The last thing I wanted to do was fight; I'm small and really had no problems with anyone in there. I just wanted to keep quiet, be left pretty much alone, and get the hell out of here.

Oh no. Apparently, Gramps hadn't settled all his internal demons earlier that morning. Here he came for his après-breakfast Round Two. I covered my eyes, ears, nose, and throat the best I could with the skimpy, threadbare Butte County–issued blanket. The stench almost cut through and overtook the vise-clamp pain in my head, but the headache proved to be superior in its needs, even through the war zone inches away. No cover—it was a fusillade of horror. I felt like the guys who would later be portrayed in *Saving Private Ryan* as they stormed the beach. Sights, sounds, terror, agony.

I read and I thought and I pondered and I worried. Had it really only been twenty-four hours since I entered this place? Could I do this ninety more times? Could I do this *one* more time? It was cramped, humid, and stuffy. Literally no escape. I just sat in my one spot for the next few hours.

Finally, I felt the now familiar rustlings of lunchtime approaching. I had been quite constipated up until now. Not that I really minded that—I had no plans to sit down in the middle of this room full of strangers and take a crap anyway. But at last, nature came calling. I concocted a brilliant plan. When the lunch group began to gather by the doors, I stayed back.

I waited until the last vestiges of the prisoners disappeared down the hallway and then beelined to the toilet (no toilet-bowl protective sheets) in the now-desolate cell. I knew I wasn't missing any gourmet fare, and the peace and quiet were actually pleasant. I felt a bit of space. I began my business. Damn, I was feeling smart. If only I could've procured a sports page, I'd have been a genius.

Just then, in the semi-bliss of my privacy, I look up and directly into the eyes of one of my jailers. I supposed they had done a head count. Heck, I was new to all of this. Maybe he thought I was lying back here having been beaten to death. Maybe he just wanted to take a private shit. Maybe he was going to search for Bob's stash. Who knows?

This was more awkward than if I had done what all the other eleven guys did quite regularly several times a day. Even the guard seemed embarrassed. I don't think anyone else had ever before given a shit about wanting a shit in solitude.

He looked at me, rather startled, and said, "You okay?" So I even had to converse during this horridly awkward moment. I nodded, and thankfully he went back to his other duties.

I finished up mine. Soon the guys came back, and everyone seemed to comfortably shit (and piss) at will right there in front of everyone else, and mere inches from my face

It was now Thursday evening, the most active party night in Chico. As I told you before, Chico State was then rated the number one party school in the country. No veteran student made an early class schedule for Friday morning. Thousands of young men and women hit the streets, heading straight to raucous parties. Huge Victorian houses hosted hundreds of souls at a time. Much drinking was accomplished. If you tired of the scene at one party, you just staggered next door to a repeat scenario. Loud, innocent, celebratory festivities. It was hard to imagine this sort of thing was taking place mere miles from where I lay. Lay very lonely, I might add.

Chapter 23: Hit the Road Jack

March 31, 1978. Friday Morning. 48 hours in.

Moving Day! I got the notice as soon as I woke up: I was gonna make the trip down to the Big House. Like my childhood dream of being called up to the big leagues—California Medical Facility at the Vacaville State Prison. It was a forty-five-minute drive away.

Let's get this shit show on the road, I thought to myself.

The sooner I began this ridiculous "agreement" made by the Butte County judge, the DA, our ineffectual lawyer, and the unpleasant probation officer who seemed to be driving this train, the better. I could ostensibly be back in the Butte County Jail in thirty days, all signed, sealed, and laden with promising recommendations, proffering up my immediate release. With my book in hand and my jail-issued clothes falling down my ass, I was led down the hallway and out into the transfer area, basically the reverse of the way I'd come in here only forty-eight hours previously.

After a pat down, they led me to the outdoors. Fresh air! Sunshine! The world actually did exist. A gravel parking lot had never looked so delightful. I almost wanted to kiss the ground. I didn't know if it was better to absorb this wonderment or just keep my senses dulled. I chose sun and air, soaking it up until I was cuffed.

Yes, handcuffed again in the back seat of a patrol car. Not only was it uncomfortable, but it was rather dangerous, when you thought about it. No seatbelts, so you would fall to the right and left during turns, and forward with your hands behind you if there happened to be an abrupt stop. (In fact, some officers in good ol' Florida used to put handcuffed prisoners in the back of the paddy wagons and drive them recklessly around town, stopping and starting and turning haphazardly. A few people died as a result. It was called a "rough ride." Lovely.) The only good thing you could say was that it was probably a good abs workout. The drive would normally be about an hour. There were two cops in front, and lo and behold, next to me was another convict sharing my ride. We had an Uber pool going, but we were headed to the same destination.

This guy looked very much like I did; not only did we have the same outfits on, but he was about the same age. We had a similar build, although he was a bit pale and wore glasses. He seemed very familiar with the cops—he was on a first-name basis. He was also very talkative. I soon learned (like, within seconds) that he had been locked up in solitary confinement for the past seven months while his case was being tried. He was a drug dealer. Things had gotten out of hand during a drug-inspired frenzy, and he had used a shotgun to blow his best friend's head off. Hey, maybe there *was* a drug issue in these parts. I hadn't heard of his case. Maybe I would've been more temperate in my actions, because, if not for the grace of God . . .

Of course, I didn't own a gun. Never have, never will. I wasn't prone to letting myself get that out of control with drugs, and I wasn't violent. If anything like the horrible story I was listening to had ever happened to me, I'd feel as bad as the guy whose head got blown off. Well, almost. It might have actually felt better than this headache. Maybe a toss-up.

Nah. I'd feel ruined. I mean, murder is an irreversible game changer. You cannot take that one back. I certainly wouldn't be jabbering in the back seat of a police cruiser with some guy I just met, cracking jokes with the two cops up front, if I'd been in that position; I'd be racked with guilt and eternal remorse. I would have related to all those guilt-inducing prayers at the Jewish temple during the High Holidays. Talky Guy did seem a bit remorseful. Oh yes—he was bummed that he had to spend the next seven years at our future home.

We headed down the country road to our eventual destination right off US Highway 80. I'd been on Highway 80 many times. It was the main route from the San Francisco Bay Area to Lake Tahoe. Vacaville was an institution (a different sort) amongst all travelers (especially those with kids), who would stop and visit the iconic Nut Tree restaurant. The Nut Tree had a little train you could ride around its property and a gift shop for travelers. Plus, you would get a mini loaf of home-baked bread with your meal.

If you were continuing to Tahoe, you would bypass the outskirts of Sacramento, where you can glimpse the golden dome of the State Capitol building. Soon thereafter, you'd begin to head up through gorgeous pine-infused mountains until you finally followed a river and arrived at Lake Tahoe, one of the most beautiful lakes known to man. It is surrounded by the highest peaks of the northern Sierra Nevada mountains, which literally dip down into a nearly bottomless lake where you can see the rocks a hundred feet under the water. I've done this drive dozens of times, always with a smile on my face.

Well, not this day. This was not a car full of happiness. It was business. All was okay as long as we were on the back roads, but then we hit the highway, and it dawned on me. What if I happened to look over and see one of my parents' friends sharing the road? If, for instance, I saw the Rubensteins on the way to their Tahoe home? Oh my God! How awful would that be? As a Jewish kid in a fairly small and fairly successful circle of my parents' mostly Jewish friends, I knew this would be devastating (even more so) for my parents. The shame. A *shanda*, Yiddish for when something unfortunate happens. Heck, the word was probably already old news throughout the three Oakland temples and multiple doctors, lawyers, and businesses establishments. Rather than take the risk, I ducked my head down and looked sideways out behind my hair.

Have you ever been curious and stared into the back seat of a cop car to see the despicable human waste being carted around? That day, it was me. The looks I received were of disgust and disdain. Believe me, I felt that way about myself too.

On the other hand, this did not seem to bother my chatterbox of a ride sharer whatsoever. Thankfully, we were now about two miles from the Vacaville State Prison. Almost there. The prison sat half a mile off the freeway, on the other side of the road from the Nut Tree. No sightings of any prominent Jews from Oakland. Soon, we'd be off the highway, safely (I hoped) ensconced in a place where I didn't think any of our family friends would bump into me.

Just then, my seatmate asked if we could go the bathroom. I thought it was a joke and would be treated as such. I mean, we were two minutes from the prison! But, to my astonishment, the county constables readily agreed to pull over at a gas station. *You've got to be fucking kidding me.* Twenty years in the future, I wouldn't even stop for my toddler-aged children under these conditions. Yet here we were, slowing down and pulling into a very busy Chevron station (like the one in *Back to the Future* where the attendants smile, whistle, and check your oil) at the parking lot of the Nut Tree herself! This was nuts. I was in disbelief, certain I was destined to run into the Isaacs or the Bermans or the Goldbergs. All I could think was: a) *Please don't let anyone that I know see me*; and b) *This has got to be a setup involving an elaborate escape attempt with shoot-outs, helicopters, and hostage-taking. News at ten!*

Wanting it to be clear that I had nothing to do with this plot, I hunkered nearly into the floorboards, head down. I did fantasize that maybe, if I could save a cop and become a hero, I'd be released.

My new "friend" was let out to do his thing. Imagine being a customer in the lavatory when a half-handcuffed man wearing a Butte County Jail ensemble enters your space. When I was politely asked if I too needed to go, I just as politely shook my head "no"—for the future escape trial, I wanted to be known as cooperative.

I waited inside the back of that car for what seemed like an eternity, listening for the inevitable first shots of the forthcoming shoot-out. I tuned my ears and cocked my head for the *whoop whoop* of the hijacked helicopter that would swoop in, poised myself for the shotguns that would shatter the car windows behind me and the yells to "COME ON!" Yet I heard none of this.

Then I dared to look up. I witnessed a placid filling station, customers going on about their business. There were smiles and a friendly atmosphere. It looked like I was watching a 1950s' movie of a happy service station through the cop car windows, while I was currently in the Twilight Zone. These simple acts were so divergent to my current experience. How I wished to simply need some gas. Or a snack. Or the public restroom. I longed to be on my way to Tahoe like I had been so many other times on this free and simple Friday. I envied those passengers. I wanted to be in any one of those other cars.

Well, there wasn't a shootout. No escape attempt either. More important, I wasn't spotted by any Jewish *yentas*. But before the murderer-pisser would return, I heard a voice that interrupted the reverie in my head, which was lodged between my thighs like they taught you in 1960s nuclear attack drills. I picked my skull up a bit to see a seven- or eight-year-old kid who looked a lot like little Ricky Beren had at that age. He was staring into the back seat of the car. The back doors were open to facilitate an easier escape, I suppose.

Little Ricky took the cherry-flavored Tootsie Pop out of his mouth and said, à la Beaver Cleaver, "Hey, mister. What are you doing in there?"

Aha! A question for the sages. One I would ask myself hundreds, if not thousands, of times in the next few months.

"He can't talk," said my guardian.

"Is he a bad guy?"

This kid could definitely become a Jungian psychologist one day. Yet another question I would ponder over the many months and years to follow.

And just like that, my murderous buddy clambered back into the car. I gave the kid my harshest sideways, squinty-eyed Clint Eastwood *I-been-wronged* look, then followed it up with a tough-guy nod to convey that he should not ever find himself in the back seat of a police vehicle. Also to express that, at age twenty-two, I was not quite the finished product I intended to be in life.

With my seatmate back, we traveled the next ten minutes to Vacaville. This is where all convicted felons from throughout California are taken to be inducted into the system—kind of like going to the draft board, which I had in 1973 with a couple of buddies. Luckily, the war had just about been over. I had always had plans to go to Canada instead of Vietnam. One of my idols, Muhammad Ali, said it best: "I ain't got no quarrel with them Vietcong."

Uneventfully, we traversed the less-than-two miles away from the highway, crossing empty fields until I saw an ominous cluster of structures ahead. The buildings were grayish brown and made of thick stone. The first thing that struck me was that the huge property was entirely surrounded by a twenty-foot-high mesh fence. On top of that fence was another three to four feet of barbed wire. The next eye-opener was the towers, which looked similar to regional airport radar stations. They were interspersed about fifty yards apart, all along the top of the fence. You could make out one or two men in each, and in each glass-encased tower you could clearly see that each man held a huge rifle. They were perfectly angled for wiping out anything they felt like within a half mile, yet they were all pointed at me—well, me and the blithering idiot in the backseat with me. Nobody looked very happy. If there had been a mirror near me, I'm sure I would have been in sync with them.

The main gate was like a checkpoint in a Communist country. A dozen uniformed guards clustered around us, with two of those sentry air-traffic controller situations directly over us. A lot of weapons were pointed in our direction. Even Chatty Charlie in the back with me was finally quiet. I guess his escape attempt had failed. Unless there was a copter headed our way right now (which would be extremely poor timing), it looked like, without further ado, we were destined to enter this place. All our backstage credentials seemed to be in order. It was time to meet the band.

Our car moved forward another fifty feet or so, and we entered an entirely enclosed chamber. The gates closed off behind us before the gate in front of us could open, sealing us into one sector before we were able to move forward into another. I felt like a salmon being guided upstream through the man-made fish ladders in Alaska, destined to be decapitated and canned.

It was just another typical Friday morning here, and a beautiful one at that. There are mountains surrounding this valley enclave; I'd driven carefree past this place dozens of times without giving a thought to what lay here. The mountains are more like rolling hills, carpeted in kelly-green grasses from the winter rains. The natural oak trees are robust and grand. I wondered what the Native Americans had been doing on this exact spot a mere 150 years before. Looking at the building, I was brought back from the beauty outside the perimeter of the fences to the chilly current usage of this land. It was an unfriendly environment. I wondered what would stand here 150 years from then.

The car pulled up to the entrance of one of the buildings, and the back doors opened for us. We were helped out, uncuffed, and bid goodbye. Now, we were officially the property of Vacaville State Prison.

I entered into a concrete room with a few benches and some open shower stalls in the corner, similar to my junior-high gym class locker room. Both these structures had been built in the early 1960s. Both had been designed to torture, humiliate, and withstand many uncomfortable men passing through their doors. And like my junior-high gym-class locker room, this would be an area where public nudity was embarrassing and mandatory.

I was ordered to strip. I felt so vulnerable. The benches were concrete. I took off my clothes down to my underwear, somewhat relieved that I was wearing boxer shorts.

"All the way!" I heard, and slowly followed the command. "Now, turn around and spread your cheeks."

I had a lot of trepidation. So far, no incident. Fuck. This was state prison. Here I was, butt naked and bent over with my ass cheeks spread wide. What was in store for me now?

This was a different version of "March Madness." It turns out that I got off with a flashlight probe (no contact, no foul) and a directive to go stand by the far wall. When my murdering failed-escape friend passed his spread-ass-cheek search, we were, without warning, blasted with a sweet, fragrant chemical spewed from a fire hose, which covered us from head to toe. The setting for a comfortable temperature did not seem of concern. (I heard later that Alcatraz was the only prison at that time with warm water. It was so that if anyone tried to escape, their body would not be accustomed to the freezing waters surrounding the prison. Boy. These dudes think of everything once someone is locked up. How 'bout they think of things to *keep* people from getting locked up?)

Shivering and stinking, we were now pronounced "deloused" and motioned toward the next attraction. Here we were met by an attendant standing behind a counter. He sized us up and plopped down an ensemble for us to try on. Our very own personal shopper, just like they have at Neiman Marcus—except his taste began and ended at blue jeans, T-shirt, green work shirt (important later, so pay attention), and socks, with the requisite "Property of Vacaville State Prison" stenciled on each piece. For some bizarre reason, they had no shoes for me, so I was once again told to continue wearing my Famolare "Get Theres." I took it as a sign, hopefully a good one. Maybe I'd just be here a very short time. Nobody else wore their outside shoes.

I marched past yet another guard area. These were always thick-glass-and-steel-windowed rooms with guards controlling the entry to each section. In this one, I noted a smiling sergeant. He was accompanied by a couple of seemingly content prisoners. One was reading the Green Pages. If you're from Northern California, you know the Green Pages are sacred. They're like the Torah. They were handed down toilet to toilet each morning in my house from when I was age ten and throughout my teens, always beginning with my father. I'd knock on his bathroom door and usually get the okay to proceed and retrieve the sports section, holding my breath as I entered and exited (and keeping my eyes down so as not to experience what else might be occurring during these recovery operations). Often, my brother swiped it out of my hands on my way down the hallway, seizing not only the newspaper but also the toilet. I had to wait to devour what Willie Mays and the rest of the Giants had done the day before. There was almost no other way to know.

My dad would say (as I dodged the poisonous fumes and horrific sights), "Mays did good last night!" That would be my first hint of what Willie and the rest of the Giants had done the night before. I'd stay up as late as I could, listening on my transistor radio (with the earplug in so my mom wouldn't hear and take it away) to hall-of-fame announcers Lon Simmons and Russ Hodges. But I'd always fall asleep during those late night broadcasts; often I'd wake up with the plug still in my ear, news (nothing like today's) or a commercial for Earl "I will paint any car for $19.99" Scheib blaring into my ear.

I also listened to rock 'n' roll (in its infancy) on local stations with that trusty AM/FM radio. The FM switch was not used until the late sixties, when the precursor to all FM free-form rock 'n' roll, KSAN, began broadcasting unheard-of album cuts from the hippie epicenter, San Francisco. KSAN was born in 1967 during the Summer of Love. Before then, I heard a healthy dose of hits on AM stations KYA and KFRC, and on KDIA "Lucky 13," where Sly of Sly and the Family Stone was a DJ. Sly was from my hometown of Oakland! How lucky we were. I got my soul indoctrination.

Meanwhile, once I got that sports page, I'd devour it. If only I had paid half as much attention to my schoolwork as I had to dissecting the stats of Mays, McCovey, and Juan Marichal, I could've challenged Einstein, Oppenheimer, or Hawking for a spot as one of the greatest minds ever. I was more interested in being the greatest center fielder ever. Years later, I even named my dog "Mays." A friend of Mr. Mays told him that I had, to which he said, "Oh. Maybe I should name my dog Beren." Ha! Classic Willie—the "Say Hey" kid.

All that to say, this sentry-guard place looked almost normal. I mean, "normal" was a different thing in my vernacular for now. I wanted a place to be safe and positive for my jacket to Butte County.

My "jacket," you ask? No, not one of the cool "Members Only" jackets that hung in my closet back in Chico, where I had a friend staying at my place and taking care of my dog. (He did both horribly, by the way.) I guess your "jacket" in jail is derived from what's on you. It's prison lingo for the information report they compile about you. I wanted a good jacket to bring back to the formal sentencing back in Butte County. I was told that working and staying out of trouble would be looked upon favorably. I guess that mantra applied both in or out of jail. Maybe the fact that I needed to be told such a thing was one of the reasons I was in this position to begin with. I could be dense at times.

Now, taking a big chance, I stepped outside the lines again and asked the guy reading the sports section, "How did the Giants do last night?"

With surprise, he asked, "Can you read?"

"Of course I can read," I answered, for the first time since second grade.

"Do you want to work here? You can read the paper every day," came the response. Damn. Easiest job interview ever.

They wrote down my cell number—not my cell phone number, my cellblock number—on a piece of paper, and made arrangements for me to report to this same spot first thing tomorrow morning. This was at the communications center of this side of the prison. Messages were taken from rotary phones, handwritten, and dispatched and delivered by a messenger, who would now be me. Wow. This was gonna be a cinch. I was going to be the best inmate ever. The bar was low, but damn it, I was gonna be the guy everyone thinks of when they say, "He was a model prisoner." I just hoped it wouldn't be printed in my obituary (or worse, in Herb Caen's column) near those coveted Green Pages in the *San Francisco Chronicle*. Plus, even with no radio or TV, I would still be able to follow my beloved Giants!

Things were moving along. They brought me to a cellblock down a hallway hundreds of feet long and forty feet wide. This corridor's floor was gleaming as if no one had anything to do but sweep and polish it day after day at seven cents an hour. Wait.

Upon arrival at the check-in area to my particular cellblock, I was informed that I had just missed lunch. Nobody really seemed to worry—more like nobody seemed to give a shit. I was shown to the television waiting room area across from the dining area. This was where, after every meal, our entire several-hundred-prisoner cellblock had to be locked in to wait for all the silverware that had been distributed during the meal to be counted, in case any pieces (most notably, knives and forks) were missing. These (along with just about anything you could think of) could be whittled or melted down into weapons. This after-meal count usually took about an hour.

I entered this room and moved to grab a seat as inconspicuously as possible. No noise, no eye contact, no (outward) fear. I was stealth. It was like the boarding area before you get on a plane, except nobody was going anywhere anytime soon. *Pretend your flight was delayed. Extremely delayed. The people here are in that sort of mood.*

It took me a few rows to find a suitable seat. Now, I didn't know that if you passed someone, you might somehow offend them. Or if you sat next to someone, you might piss someone else off. It's an entire pile of shit to be determined. I did not focus or linger on any one person or any group of people, but I knew that I was being monitored.

When I figured (and I really had no idea) it was appropriate to lift my head and gaze over the room, I was met by a fairly friendly face. I nodded slightly and politely, and he smiled. All good—except there were no teeth in his head. I just kept my look even and slowly turned toward another seat. There, another inmate was smiling (with all his teeth). As he turned toward me, it exposed a massive scar that looked like a cheap zipper running from his neckline to his ear. It was thick and oozy and looked like it could pop open at any second—definitely not performed by a Beverly Hills board-certified plastic surgeon. This was kind of interesting, but I was keeping my best Mr. Spock face on.

Speaking of faces: as casually as possible, I looked around during those next thirty minutes or so, never resting on any face for any amount of time but looking just long enough to see things that you didn't often see in the outside world. Every face had a scar or a tattoo or an indicator of a different path that had brought it here. The eyes (if both were intact) were filled with pain, despair, anger, and fear. Well, mine were afraid. I felt like Luke in the famous *Star Wars* bar scene, where everyone is from a different galaxy and the atmosphere is extremely tense. Normally when you enter a room (or a bar), you look around and everyone looks like someone you've seen before. There's a familiarity. Sometimes you even see people you actually know. Here, there was little chance for that, at least for me. These guys looked nothing like anyone I had known or seen before. It was truly as if I had landed on another planet—one with no familiar, comforting, or particularly friendly faces.

After lunch, we were allowed to go off to our various ways of spending time. Some guys went directly to the medical side of the facility to receive their various doses of medications. These guys had permission to travel down the long, spotless hallways. Vacaville had a pretty advanced medical facility. I saw many people in various stages of transitioning. This was an entirely foreign concept to me. Me being a white, urban kid, I thought I was cool, but I was practically living in a vacuum of unawareness. Inmates wearing bras and full makeup, with long hair and painted fingernails, strutted proudly about. I had no idea. I still have no idea. I did no research on Vacaville. I wasn't interested. My only goal was to get the fuck outta there as soon as possible. I was just an observer in that habitat, truly a fish out of water and way beyond my depth.

People also had jobs to do and business to take care of. There was always some sort of hustle going on. As dense as I was, I could feel it all around me. There were tight knots of guys in deep conversation. I wasn't any part of it, and that was fine, but there was always an underlying tension. Men went off to work in the kitchen; these dudes never went hungry. And there was laundry duty, maintenance, gardening. Most of the men went outside to the yard. This wasn't for their benefit; it was so the prison guards could just put everyone in one area and monitor them more easily.

I followed the majority of our cellblock out to the yard. It was a massive grass field, probably half a mile by another half a mile in size. There was a baseball diamond and several tracks for running (or mostly endless walking, and always in the same direction) around the perimeter of the field. In one large section, there was a sand pit with heavy steel weights and pull-up bars. This was occupied by men of behemoth stature, pulling and grunting and crashing the weights down and yelling. I steered very clear of this area—these guys looked like they could lift cars if they chose to.

There were a few full-court basketball games being played. The voices were loud and the play was fast. It was all punctuated by a lot of street talk and vigorous shrieks of, surprisingly, laughter! These guys were (or at least seemed to be) having a fabulous time. I couldn't understand. I was miserable.

This could've been like gym class at my large high school, the difference being we were all now surrounded by those high fences with those air-traffic-control-tower-type nests looking over us. In each sector were two to four guards. Most importantly, they had huge weapons pointed at me and my compadres. The guards all wore dark sunglasses. I had no idea what they were thinking or where their eyes were looking. Who's to say one of them couldn't just pull off a round into you at any moment?

I figured I could get along with everyone out here. Growing up in Oakland, California, we were pretty well integrated in my schools from my third grade on. We white kids grew up having plenty of Black friends and plenty of Black guys (and girls) we didn't like—same for white and Hispanic and Asian kids. You liked or disliked people for who they were first, not what race, religion, or whatever else they were. It was great. A very fortunate way to grow up.

I followed the crowd like a sheep—a white one. I mostly kept to myself and clomped along with everyone else. Eventually, I found myself in step beside a Black guy. Just to be cordial, I initiated a casual conversation. Nothing deep or personal, just "Hey how's it going?"– type stuff. He gave me a sideways glance and just shrugged. I agreed. That about said it all.

The rest of the afternoon, I sat out on the lawn, alone. Lost in my thoughts. I watched the basketball games from a safe distance away so I wouldn't be chosen to play. Basketball is not my best sport. Later on in my real life, while I was shooting an episode of *Cheers*, I tossed up a shot from just beyond the three-point arc in a gym filled with friends. Somehow, with twenty balls being hoisted toward the same bucket, none other than Hall of Famer Kevin McHale (guest-starring in that week's episode) picked up my errant shot, effectively rendering the gym silent, and pronounced me "not only the worst basketball player here, but the worst basketball player I've ever seen." That comment was followed by gales of laughter.

That sound was not very far off from the ones I was hearing here around me. The guys were having an actual . . . well, ball. I did not share those emotions; I was more of an emotional wreck. So I watched.[2]

After a few hours had passed, I almost thought of closing my eyes and drifting off. I had been up since 5:00 a.m. It had been a rather harrowing day—I mean, with those obviously thwarted escape attempts, and that nude decontamination procedure to assure we had no contagions. I had landed a job, though! I looked around. Not many sunbathers. I wasn't really in the kick-back, "Hey, I'm on a beach in the Bahamas right now" kind of mood anyway. Plus, I still had a gigantic migraine. I pondered if it would have felt better had those guards filled my head with hot lead from some of those shotguns, rather than letting me suffer what was going on in there at the moment. No sleep. High anxiety. Bright lights. Loud noises. No food. No coffee. No medication. No Bahamas vacation. Oh yeah, lots of fear, and I was smoking a cigarette every twenty minutes or so. No relief in sight. Would those guns even end this pain?

It appeared some type of activity was being throughout the huge field. Without preamble, the herd began migrating in the same general direction. I was thinking gang fight, mass prison breakout now for sure. Everyone else appeared fairly mellow, especially when such a potentially breaking news story on CNN was brewing—even though CNN had not been invented yet. It would be invented for this, though!

Three bells sounded in quick succession. I guessed that was the warning that the snipers were on to us and their weapons were fully, uh, weaponized. Still, it was a seemingly organized rebellion. No false

---

2   This was similar to another time later in my free life, when I found myself on the famed Venice, California, basketball courts where they were filming *White Men Can't Jump*. There was lots of smack talk and lots of great players (some former NBA and NCAA stars), and lo and behold: just like in the movie, Wesley Snipes asked me to team up with him against Woody Harrelson, Ted Danson, and George Wendt, with whom I had driven down to visit the set. Woody, Ted, George, and I had a running game (Ted and me vs. Woody and George) for years before shows. They knew how terrible I was. Let's just say my play did not go as well as Woody's in the film. I wish I had sat out that afternoon also.

moves, no quick "Run for it" or "Yeah, we got this"—all in stride. I wondered where I would head once the revolution was over. Mexico? Nah, maybe Canada. *I can join the draft dodgers.* (They hadn't been pardoned yet. I felt their cause.)

Reality turned out to be somewhat less dramatic—I quickly learned from one of the brief and mumbled answers to my questioning that we were off to our cellblocks to await (always) dinner. It was 3:45 p.m.

After we exited the yard, we all had to merge into a completely caged-in walking area (no guards) some fifty yards long. Think of a zoo when they want to move the dangerous animals from one area to another, except some of *these* animals had homemade weapons. Guys brushed up against one another. Tensions could get high. This was not a good place to have an enemy. It would take a while for anyone to assist you in case of an emergency—that is, assuming anyone wanted to hurry and assist you. I put my head down, kept my distance, and found myself fed into a grand assembly area, much like an airport terminal. In this case, there were no signs indicating exotic destinations where you're to go. I was assigned to Cellblock A. (At least I was getting one "A" this semester.) I found the area without much trouble. This place hadn't really been designed for geniuses to get around, so at least I was up to speed on this account. Also, we had the guards to guide us.

Ah, the guards. This was a strange collection of people. Who would gravitate toward a job (career?) where you effectively spend a third of your life in prison? There are no upsides to this profession in my book. You're not a police officer who could one day rescue a little kitty out of a tree and hand it back to a six-year-old girl in pigtails—no, you are dealing only with a bad segment of humanity. The dregs of society. Angry men. And there is no arena of rehabilitation to hope for; it's merely monitoring and maneuvering nasty prisoners from one area to another.

I did have a little bit of interaction with a few of my captors, and they were mostly pretty good guys. Hell, I lived, didn't I? One guard in Vacaville was very kind, and a couple of jailers and patrol officers in Butte County were nice too. I did have one older guard in the county jail who took a particular dislike to me, and I reciprocated the feeling, enough to say some very dumb shit to him—more on that later.

Yes, I said things that were stupid, immature, and dangerous to spout off. But let me just say it here and now: After spending some time in prison, I feel differently about the system. Some people *belong* in jail. I was glad that many of the people I met there were locked away from most of the people I knew and loved in the mostly free world. The operative word here is *many*. These people had no real intention of re-entering the general population and becoming upstanding citizens—at least, from the stories I had heard them tell, I thought they should have been kept away from my family. Especially the children I did not yet have. I would argue that some should have been locked up forever, or more. And I believe it should not have been in such a country club. But these guys were having a blast. Why *not* go out and commit crimes, come in here, and have a party? They were served three meals a day. They had a relatively comfortable bed. There were toilet facilities (private ones in your own room in Vacaville). *And* you could watch television (you just couldn't turn the channel, or a deadly riot could break out). There were even movie nights (5:30 p.m.) on Saturdays. There was access to advanced medical care (sometimes cutting edge, if you were cut by an inmate) and a library, which was seldom used. Just like on the outside. Outdoors was playtime, and the guys had many friends (and family members) in here from their free lives at home.

The remorse factor seemed quite low—about 0 percent. Here the blame centered squarely on the victims. It was quite a new perspective for me. Although here I was blaming Butte County, so who the fuck am I to talk? But I felt quite differently. Maybe it was the Jewish guilt. Now, I understand I come from privilege. In fact, it could be construed that I was the worst offender of this lot. I had the most opportunities and still ended up here. I was worse than anyone around me. I was feeling awful for everyone whom I had disappointed (save for the narc I shorted on the quarter gram). And I felt bad even before I ended up doing prison time. These guys did not feel one bit of regret (at least, not from what they said) for the pain they caused others. I did not want to see them get out and interact with any of the people I cared about. This rang true for about 65 percent of the people I dealt with, which is about the same as the recidivism rate for prisoners returning to the system within three years in California. I am excluded from all that, of course.

Now, I get that there has always a segment of society that views breaking laws differently than other groups in that same society. I admit I was in the group that defied the law. My lawlessness was part "white privilege"—I felt I could get away with my crimes. But I also felt I was perpetuating a "victimless" crime. Nothing ever violent. I would never steal or harm anyone.[3] I guess there is a certain attraction to being an outlaw. I don't share it. Hollywood has made a killing off of it. In the movies, I always feel the entire issue could be solved if they would just tell the police.

I don't understand why some people become police, but I admire them—some of them. I could never do it. Some of these people are crooks themselves. I guess that's why in the movies you can't always go to the police—some cops like to stop the crooks, and some like to hang around the crooks. I didn't want any part of it. I was miserable. My mind was careening inside itself at a thousand miles per hour. I was exhausted. It was still only my first day here—actually, my first few hours here.

---

3   In fact, one time I was in a fistfight with one of my best friends a week before my bar mitzvah. I was winning handily. All our gang (we were twelve-year-old Jewish boys) was watching. As I was slugging him, I felt terrible. (Not as bad as I would have felt if he had ever connected with me, because weighing in at about ninety pounds, he would've killed me.) His mom, who was at our house at the time, looked out of the window and saw us across the street on her lawn. She screamed, and the parents all ran over. I was so glad when they stopped it. I hated to fight.

We all went back to the silverware counting room—pre-counting, I guess. This was before dinner, and this time they were counting us to see if anyone escaped the fortress during the past hour. We were counted dozens of times a day, every fifteen minutes. Afterward, we were emptied across the hallway and into the dining room. I guess they had our reservations, and our orders. Guards lined the room. There were about fifty tables seating four each. Everything was bolted to the floor.

We lined up and made our way to the buffet. Inmates behind the counters portioned out the meal evenly to each passing prisoner. Even though I could've vomited from the nausea caused by my migraine, I found myself pretty hungry. I ate my surprisingly good meal with absolutely no interaction. We were dismissed one table at a time to bus our trays and head back to the waiting area/TV room to be head-counted yet again—but more importantly, to have the utensils all present and accounted for back in the kitchen area.

It was now about 5:00 or 6:00 p.m. I noticed the dearth of clocks, like a casino. The count seemed to have been successful, but who knew—maybe I could get spooned tonight (I hoped not, in any capacity). We were led back into the dining area, now spotless. Somehow transistor radios appeared at several tables. They were immediately set to the highest volume, the dial turned up so high on the small radios that the sound became mostly distortion. The music choices on each radio were in direct conflict with each other. There was Christian music, rock 'n' roll, soul and country and gospel and pop. It was eventually just loud noise.

Cards, dice, and domino tiles magically arrived. It was like a carnival. There was gambling, shouting, crashing of domino tiles, and again, those peals of laughter. It was like we were on a cruise ship. I sat stunned. And mute. And glum. I did not participate in any of the festivities. I was not in a very celebratory mood, and I could not understand how these guys could be. I looked around the room. These laughing men had ruined many lives. Innocent lives. I didn't care much about their own. That had been their choice. It was those innocent victims I mourned.

After an hour or so, it seemed as if the indoor version of playtime was over. All the toys got packed up, and we were filtered out into the main corridor and off to our homes for the night. It was about 7:00 p.m. or so, and I was ready to crash out. We trudged up the metal staircase single file, up the three floors to my level. Then I carefully walked two-thirds of the way down the catwalk to my cell. The aisle was no more than three feet wide, and the guardrail was barely higher than three feet. I had to pass various criminals to get to my place. All metal and cement. I looked over the railing to the cement floor, trying to see where I might land after being tossed over the rail.

At last, I stood outside my closed, thick, steel address. This was where I would reside for the next however long it took to get me out of this place. There was a one-foot-by-one-foot window in my door. The bottom of the door had about six inches open so they could throw stuff in at you, like mail—or food if there was a riot, which I expected every other second. The window was so they could shine a flashlight into your eyes every thirty minutes or so during the night.

We all lined up outside our doors. Next to me, about five feet away, there was a guy about my age—I guess you could call him "my neighbor." We nodded to each other. He spoke first, introducing himself as Terry. He was pretty intelligent, I could tell right away, and he seemed fairly normal. He was very comfortable in his surroundings. He'd obviously been here before. We exchanged a few pleasantries, and then with a loud electric buzz the entire floor of very heavy doors opened at once. That was the cue for our entire group of men to step forward and enter. I wished my new buddy good-night, and with that, I walked into my state prison cell for the first night. It was 7:30 p.m. It had been a lo-o-ong day.

It didn't take me very long to tour my habitat. I did have a window—barred, of course—that measured about two feet by six inches, out of which I could see parts of this vast prison complex. I wondered what one would do if he were in actual, desperate medical need. What if there were a fire? Or I were being assaulted? There was virtually no way to call for help. Men wailed incessantly throughout the night, so one more scream would have meant little. And if any help was coming, it would take a long time to arrive. I was basically on my own.

Fortunately, I was exhausted. I noted the steel toilet; I took in the metal desk and cement black stool. I hopped up to my bunk, which was about five feet high and rested on top of a solid hunk of cement. I found myself in a little space with about one to two feet of room between me and the cement ceiling. It was like I was in an MRI chamber, perhaps more claustrophobic.

I did not sleep very well this night. First of all, it was about 8:00 p.m. on a Friday night. That's about two hours before we used to begin our evening. I also had a lot on my mind, of course. But more than that, the various jungle-like shouts and shrieks were discomforting. Plus, there was the quarter-hourly flashlight to the eyes through the little window in the door to interrupt that REM sleep pattern. The window was for the guards to constantly check to see if anyone had escaped from his crypt.

Chapter 24: The Fool on the Hill

APRIL 1, 1978. THE NEXT DAY.

Yes, it was April Fools' Day. The meaning of this date is not lost on me. I did feel like a fool.

It was Saturday—early, about 6:00 a.m. It had been a while since I had been up on a Saturday morning at 6:00 a.m., unless I had been up partying the entire night before, but I had to go with the flow. The clattering of the farm animals was beginning. They were arising. However weak it may have been, I'd missed yesterday's coffee window, and I'd slept horrifically, coupled with smoking on and off all night. Jesus. What if I (or anyone else) accidentally set their mattress on fire? It wouldn't be pretty. My head was ready to explode. It ached incessantly. The clamoring and clanking of metal meeting cement in a harsh crescendo of sharp noises did nothing to ease my pain. No aspirin at the ready. I didn't even know how I could get any. What kind of two-bit drug dealer was I? I couldn't even score a Bayer.

I did manage to peel off a minor bowel movement. All by myself! In my private little toilet/master bedroom/office suite. You sure do appreciate the little things when your freedom is vastly reduced.

At precisely 6:15 a.m. (I guess—I've never worn a watch), all the cells automatically unbolted and slid open. We were instructed to step forward and stand in front of our now automatically shut cell doors. It was a glorious sunny morning, early spring. I looked ahead from my third-story perch, near the dead end of a hundred-yard-long tier. There were hundreds of lime-green-dressed inmates standing in front of their lime-green doors. I gave a nod to my friend Terry on my immediate left, then looked to my right.

Upon turning my neck ninety degrees (which I could do more easily in those days), I saw the sun had now been preempted by the figure that stood outside the door three feet from me. I do not think I had ever seen a larger human being in my life. He must have stood well over 6′10″ and was nearly as wide, except at the waist, which was thirty inches—the same size as each of his biceps. If you've seen Michelangelo's *David* in its full seventeen-foot actual size, you'll catch my drift, except this guy's head was completely shaved, and I had not seen his penis yet (although I was sure that if he wanted me to, that would happen). *It was nice knowin' ya*, I thought.

I looked over the railing and saw that my landing spot was still available, should he decide he wanted to casually swat me over with a brush of one of his tree-trunk arms on his way to breakfast. However, Lionel—that was his name—oblivious to my quadruple take, split not my skull but his face into the most gleaming smile I had encountered to that point or would encounter since. It re-lit the cellblock. Whew![4]

Off we went to breakfast. Lionel must've arrived in the middle of the previous night. He was mostly smiling and talking to me in the sweetest, slowest Southern drawl. I liked this guy. He was so damn nice. God knows why he was in there, and I wasn't about to ask. At this point, I felt safe in his presence, but he was immediately gobbled up by another clique. He had the brawn—he needed the brains. Inside-type brains. I hoped they wouldn't take undue advantage of him. They immediately had him moved to their area.

Back to the routine. Even though it was only my first full day, it all seemed the same. Wake up. Count. Breakfast. Count. Yard. Count.

---

4   The only feeling I can relate to this is when, much later, I was on the Paramount Studios lot (in a relatively safer environment) watching an extraordinarily beautiful girl being escorted my way by an obviously goony-walking guy. I stayed and waited to check her out more clearly; when they got closer, I realized that it was Robin Givens. By then my mind was racing, and when I looked over at the clown next to her I saw he was, of course, Mike Tyson. They both broke out laughing at my error and terror.

I lost count of the counts. Then I returned back for the pre-lunch count and was handed a paper message. I had a visitor!

I hoped this wasn't a cruel April Fools' Day joke. What I really hoped was that my visitor here would tell me that that my entire ordeal *had* been an April Fools' Day joke, and it was all over! Maybe Amber would be there with a big smile (although not as huge as Lionel's) like I hadn't seen since she had been dressed as one of the Three Blind Mice for Halloween so long ago. *Was that really only five months ago?*

I tried to act cool. I didn't want to offend or upset anyone who didn't have a visitor. I didn't know the protocol. I didn't know where to go and/or when to go there. I certainly did not want to miss this. I relied on my captors for this vital information.

"Uh. Excuse me, sir." I didn't want to upset them for fear they would end up revoking my visit (and possible release?) privileges. "I got this visitor notice. When and where and how do I go about this, sir?" To me it was the most important question since the Big Bang mystery, which hadn't even been asked yet. To everyone else it was "I couldn't give a shit."

I was met with a shrug and "You'll be notified when it's time."

I just stood there, dumbfounded. I was treated less abruptly by Steve Rubell outside the front door of Studio 54 one year later, when he positively would not let me enter for the five hours I begged. (Although he did spend an inordinate amount of time outside with me at the ropes—he on one side, me pleading to get in on the other. Makes me wonder exactly why he was out there so much and where the real party was.) It was quite festive out there on the street with the growing mob. Here, it was clear I'd rather be on the outside.

I found my buddy, Terry, who set me straight on the visitor situation. It was usually an afternoon event. Once everyone had been counted again after lunch and everything was in place (people, utensils, etc.) on the inside, those with visitors reported to a secure room. Here I would be frisked and then led to another secure room. They would give me a number; my visitor was given the corresponding number. When they called that number, I was to squeeze my way down a very tight rectangular passageway with stools on different sides of unbreakable glass partitions. On each side was a telephone receiver attached to a two-foot-long metal cord. Once I found my numbered seat, my visitor would be led into the corresponding numbered seat across from me. I'd done this before in Oroville. I hoped it wouldn't come with the ass beating I got after my visit there.

I had to wait hours for this opportunity. Imagine having something to look forward to in jail. You've got literally nothing to do to distract you or pass the time more quickly. It's agony. It felt like I was back in third grade on a Friday afternoon when you had big weekend plans, waiting on a clock that was ticking backwards. Except there were no clocks—only bells and shouts and counts.

My head still ached. No refills, and at any rate the coffee was as weak as the fight I would have put up against Mike Tyson. My cigarettes were getting dangerously low. There was no place to nap (besides, I did not want to miss my visit). There were no sports on TV. There was only a black-and-white TV bolted to a high corner to be played after the meal count. There was no music. Nor eating. I had no books. So I just sat there.

Finally! The call came to go inside for lunch. First the count, of course. I ate quickly, hoping to encourage the others to follow suit. Damn, they could take their sweet-ass time. This wasn't Le Cirque for God's sake. Back to the TV/lounge. *Oh Lord, please let this count be right.*

I waited. And waited. Oh fuck—there was a discrepancy with the count. *C'mon, fellas!* The count was repeated. Now, we're not talking about Isaac Newton doing the tabulating here. I was extra anxious about time as well—an hour had passed. I wondered who it was that was coming to visit, or if they had stayed. I really only wanted to see one person, but she was locked up God only knew where.

My mind raced. I worried. Then I remembered that I could only have one of a few preselected visitors. I could have my family and one or two others. I was grateful, but I was afraid that one of my well-meaning friends was crashing the party. I really wanted to see Brooke. I wanted to know how and where Amber was.

Okay. Something was happening. We were being brought back into the dining hall. Then we were told to line up against the walls with our faces toward the concrete. They were going to search everyone.

This is when I knew that this traffic jam was going to make me very late. This was before Waze could possibly have saved me. *Please, please, please. Just let me visit for an hour. Or a half hour. Just give me five fucking minutes! Please.* I didn't care who it was. Apparently neither did the guards or my fellow inmates. I wanted to scream, but I didn't want to attract any attention and be thought of as complicit in the silverware heist, especially now that my visit was at stake.

Against the wall I stood, nose pressed up close. In came half a dozen tactical armed guards. They were not fucking around. They began at the far side of the room. If I had that silverware, I would've shit it out. I thought this would go on forever, but everyone seemed to be well-versed in this drill. The "bulls" (I had just learned that nickname they used for guards, and now that I was a twenty-four-hour veteran I guessed I could use it too) had actually moved through about half the inmates in little more than fifteen minutes. Time did move quickly there! Especially when you were having fun!

Then I heard the guy next to me whisper in an urgent hiss, "Pass this down."

I looked to my left and saw what "this" was. It was the spoon.

This was what the guards—excuse me, the bulls—were looking for. I didn't know whose side I was on. I had absolutely no desire whatsoever to touch that object. My horrified reaction must've said that, because my comrade withdrew his generous offer. Like, what was I gonna do with it?? Eat Jell-O? Add bananas to mine please.

I did the next best thing, which was nothing. As the guards (or bulls, or bullguards, whatever they called 'em) closed in, I closed my eyes, froze, and hoped for the best. They arrived at my immediate left and quickly surrounded my non-partner in crime.

"WEAPON!" screamed one of the officers, proudly holding up the small spoon like a trophy while wearing full riot gear.

Now all six were pointing their large guns (when doesn't a pointed gun look large?) at the guy. They took him down with great precision and professionalism, then dragged him out of the area. He was cuffed and roughed up on the way out. I didn't know where to look. I didn't know if I had done the right thing. I didn't know if anyone had heard him ask me to pass the weapon (in this case, a tarnished teaspoon) along. I didn't really care. Unlike Glenn Close in *Fatal Attraction*, I wanted to be ignored. Please.[5]

Well, they had found what they were looking for. We were all allowed to move over to the TV waiting room area. And yes, there was another head count—minus me, because I was called and allowed to make haste to the visitors' area. I raced/walked toward my destination. At this point, I didn't care who was there to see me. I just knew it wasn't someone capable of trying to fob off a felonious lethal weapon (in this case a dull spoon, not even a spork) onto me.

I made it to my visit with only twenty minutes left. I wound my way past all the sad clumps of men and their separated families. I

---

5   Years later, after shooting an episode of *Cheers*, we would often go upstairs to have a few beers and play highly competitive foosball. One time, I was about to slam a ball past Woody when I glanced up to see Glenn Close standing right behind him. She and Woody were doing a play together, and she was his girlfriend for a while. I mean, who wasn't there for a bit with him?

This was right around the time *Fatal Attraction* was out—it was frightening to just see her. All the guys (except Woody, I guess) were petrified of her. Such an amazing performance. Can you imagine? Woody actually cheated on Glenn Close *after* she starred in *Fatal Attraction*.

Thing is, she was so damn nice, and super cool too. Still. Scary. No one cheated on their wives or girlfriends that night, I'm sure, except maybe for Woody. Either way, I still crushed that ball past him as he stood there helpless.

caught snippets of conversations along the way—from "Hang in there" and "I love you" to "Fuck you, bitches" and other sundry threats. At last, I arrived at my designated slot.

It was my mother! And my brother! They were a sight for sore eyes! A few moments of very stunted conversation followed. Then I asked, "Hey, where's Dad?"

I mean, he had always been my biggest advocate and constant supporter. I'm much closer to my dad than anyone else in my family. This didn't feel right. Maybe another April Fools' joke? *Maybe he's waiting with the keys to this joint. He's always been able to fix things.*

They didn't hesitate for a moment to answer my question: "Oh, he's working. You know Dad."

I did know him. He worked religiously six days a week. This was Saturday, the holiest of holy days of the retail business.

"He really wanted to be here," they continued.

I bought it hook, line, and sinker. I really am a fool. On every day of the year.

My dad *did* visit the following Wednesday, and every Wednesday after that. He also made most Sundays part of his visiting schedule, and he wrote me every day. It typically took four days to receive a letter from one hundred miles away, plus the mandatory censoring and searching for contraband adding to the delay. This was before I met Cliff Clavin, with his dedication to delivering the mail. My jailers did not share such passion.

Meanwhile, my bro and my mom tried to shore me up. Met with these efforts, and having just witnessed the spoon thief suffer more of a roughing up than I ever had (collectively) at the hands of my brother, I broke down. I sobbed. I begged them. I knew it wasn't fair, nor their fault I was there, but I just lost it. I kept crying and asked them to get me out of there. I had tried to put on a suit of armor, but it was really just soft putty.

Our visiting time was up. We knew this because suddenly the sound between us was cut off. No volume was necessary.

A few years later, I found out why my dad wasn't at the prison that first visiting day. It seems that after I was hauled away in handcuffs, he had frantically tried to reverse the decision in everyone's mind. He had continued his pleas with the district attorney and the judge in the judge's chambers for an hour. He had even lowered himself to attempt to reason with the repugnant Gustine.

Gustine took delight in positioning himself in my father's way. He had the power right now, and oh, how he was relishing it. He got to watch my elegant, sophisticated, educated father come down to his level. My dad tried to reason with this scumbag throughout my stay in jail. For his troubles, Gustine had my dad put in restraints also. I basically put my father in jail here with me.

I learned later that, after my dad's attempts to reverse my sentence, he and my mom and brother drove back to Oakland, where my father was taken to the hospital after suffering a panic attack. He was having trouble breathing and began hyperventilating. He passed out. He remained in the hospital for three days. And I thought I was having a few bad days. Poor guy. He literally ached for his son. I would not know such love until I would have children of my own.

Our visit wrapped up. No hugs and kisses goodbye, however.

My lunchtime brush with a possible additional felony (or worse) had long passed. I hoped nobody thought I had somehow been disloyal to "Spoonie," the spoon-passing guy. Who knew how the thought process went on around here? Who knew who he was connected to? Certainly not me, and I was connected to exactly no one. That was gonna change big time, though. I'll get to that later; for now, I was more worried about who had seen me blubbering like a baby to my mommy.

The rest of the Sabbath passed in a relatively mundane fashion. I almost would've preferred to spend the day at services in temple during one of the High Holidays. Boy, those suckers went on forever. I should have listened maybe?

It's interesting how a man can adapt so quickly to his environment.

When I was first locked up on that November morning, I could not imagine surviving more than the few hours that I had already been in. It had now been a few days. I was adapting. If this was to end up being a few years, though, I thought I'd go nuts. So far, it was my first Saturday night. Count. Dinner. Utensil count. Hopefully, after the strong show of police force, there wouldn't be any more attempted thefts, but you never knew with this crowd. Indoor recess, and then up to my sleep chamber. I wondered if the Incredible Hulk would change his demeanor and flick me off our tier—but, it turned out, he was no longer my neighbor.

I now had an active balance in the commissary. Thanks, Mom. I bought cigarettes, books, and some writing supplies. I began my constant reading. I traded for books and even got to check some out in the prison library. I also got down to writing some letters.

I couldn't write directly to Amber. You see, even after the explicit ban was lifted, we were encouraged (later formally sentenced for five years) not to communicate with one another. One had to secure special privileges to communicate institution to institution anyway. I requested that, but things took a while to be processed. All incoming and outgoing correspondence was monitored. I wasn't saying anything illegal to her, unless wanting to smother her to death with kisses was a crime. I wasn't plotting an escape, other than to go to a deserted island with her forever when all of this was over. I just wanted to let her know how much I missed her and loved her and felt horrible and responsible. I still couldn't believe she'd been caught up in this because of me. I wanted to send her strength and support, and to not let them emotionally and physically beat us.

The loud, plaintive wails in the cellblock died down as the herd settled in for the evening. I figured every hour that I slept was almost as good as one spent sleeping in Cabo San Lucas. Plus, upon awakening, although not in Cabo, I was that much closer to putting this nightmare (and I had plenty of those) behind. Stress dreams? How about stress-in-jail-while-actually-in-jail dreams?

Chapter 25: Sunday Bloody Sunday

Church call. Uh, I think not. I was never one to embrace religion. *Like, if there is a God, where have you been the past few months, dude?* I did wonder how large the Jewish congregation in here was. I mentioned before that as much as I really (and I mean really, really, really) did not like those three-hour-long High Holiday services at Temple Beth Abraham in Oakland, I'd gladly do the morning and afternoon services in lieu of this. At least at Temple in the 1960s during the October High Holidays, we used to bring a transistor radio and listen to the World Series with the earphone snaked up through our shirts. My dad pretended to not know what religion I was praying for, but would miraculously (as if I were God) ask me the score of the game every few innings—especially when he heard a small cheer rumble from the other little Jewish wanna-but-never-will-be Willie Mayses throughout the *shul*. Later in the early 1970s, when the Oakland A's dominated major league baseball, we did our World Series praying directly to God from our seats at the Oakland Coliseum.

Other than it being Sunday, there was little difference (in my extensive three-day prison expertise) between this and any other day in there. Wake up. Count. Food. Count. Extreme tension and more extreme boredom. TV room. Outdoor playtime. Food. Count. You get the picture. I noticed a few self-styled ministers preaching to some clusters of guys. There was some gospel singing. Then food. Count. Indoor games. But what's that? I hear it's movie night. Shit.

Now, I love a good movie, but I just didn't want to get shivved in one. Leave the murdering for the screen. What could possibly happen to me in a darkened theater closely huddled together with a bunch of killers? I found Terry and stayed close to him. But what if Terry wanted a little action in the theater? What if Lionel did? This was not good, but into the theater I went.

Turns out the "theater" was just an old gymnasium. The screen was about five feet wide (about the size of most of today's home television setups) and set up at half court. There was a projector in the middle of the audience. It was old-school AV-club style, with the film running from reel to reel. We were to sit in bleachers, a good forty feet from the screen. Everyone seemed to give each other a respectful distance. It wasn't dark outside yet, and the lights never lowered much. The guards were never far away. I still envisioned a flat-out brawl, but it did not occur. We watched *The Sentinel*, and I must say, I enjoyed it very much.

It was not very scary. What was scary was looking around and seeing myself surrounded by hundreds of the scariest guys the most imaginative screenwriters of Hollywood could possibly have for subjects. Much like on an airplane, where disasters in the air are not shown, I'm sure the content of the films was screened so as to not stir the inmates to rise up. On to beddy-bye.

Chapter 26: Monday, Monday

Our doors had these three-inch openings all across the bottom. I soon learned to wedge my feet under them and do a few sit-ups. One night I was doing a set when there came a frantic knocking on my door. I got up and looked out the little window into the face of a petrified trusty.

A trusty is a prisoner who has proven himself able to perform simple tasks that the guards either don't want to do, or . . . yeah, I guess that about sums up what the trusties did. In the ten-hour overnight shift, the guards didn't even want to get up and walk the fifty yards down the hall to count heads beyond the rest of the time sitting and doing nothing. So, this trusty was performing the quarter-hourly head count. You had to sleep with your head in one direction so they could just shine the flashlight into the window and quickly count you as a non-escapee.

These guys did not get their jobs according to their brainpower level. At that moment, I was not in my bed, and the trusty was freaking out. He thought I had escaped. If he had only stepped an inch to the left or looked down a few feet, he would have seen my toes wiggling out from the bottom of the three-inch-thick steel door. This was not the head count from the resident supervisor in a dorm at Stanford. I popped up, and his eyeballs popped back into his head.

Anyway, on this particular night, at 2:00 a.m., I awoke to the sound of a slab being tossed under one of those openings. I figured that dying by a pipe bomb thrown into one's cell would at least be quick—and I'd make headlines. Oh, wait, that wouldn't be good. Maybe I'd be so obliterated that they wouldn't be able to positively ID me for the papers. I fearfully counted to thirty, awaiting the explosion, and then tried to go back to sleep. It wasn't easy, as my heart rate must've registered over two hundred beats per minute.

Finally, I hopped out of bed, and there on the floor was a packet of letters enclosed with a rubber band! They had been sliced open by a letter opener, and I guessed that had passed the acid test. Damn. I wondered if someone would've sent me blotter acid. That could be dosed on paper. As much as I loved acid, I don't think I would have liked doing acid in prison, but it would have been quite the trip.

Either way, these letters brought me such a feeling of love. The connection to the outside world cannot be underplayed. It did exist! And I was still a part of it. Such a wonderful moment. I tore open the already-torn-open envelopes. As nice as it was for everyone (and anyone) to write, I always looked for word about or from Amber first.

I loved getting letters and am lucky to tell you that I got them every day. Sometimes I got four or five letters in the overnight express. All of them passed on encouragement, support, and love. They were funny and informative and made me want to join the authors in the future. My dad was the most prolific writer. I received a letter from him almost every day. His letters were filled with positive passages. He would give me a running narrative newsfeed about my family, friends, and his business. He always pointed out that "this too shall end," and of course, he kept me up on all the local sports teams. Basically, it was like we were sitting together. Those letters were a great way to begin each day, even though the events they described were several days past.

I'd also hear from Brooke. She was funny. She'd tell me about Amber, still disguising her by calling her "Amberly" in our extremely sophisticated code. Occasionally, I'd get a letter that Amber sent to Brooke to pass along to me; I'd process and cherish every word. She was very careful and tempered in her phrasing. As great as it was to get and receive all those letters, it also brought me down a little lower after their glow wore off. It made me miss everyone that much more. Still, again, I was lucky enough to hear the wondrous sound of paper sliding over concrete under my metal door in the middle of every night. Sometimes I'd get up to try and read the letters, but without lights (and no flashlight option on the not-yet-invented smartphones) it was not a viable option. My address was: Richard Beren: Inmate c/o Vacaville State Medical Facility, Inmate B-91593Z. Not the toniest of addresses.

I'd write back to those letters at first light. Then off to breakfast we'd go, and I'd drop the letters in the mail area.

Today, at the cellblock reception desk, I was handed a note. I was to report to my new job! I headed to the intake area where I had seen the inmate reading the sports page and the nice sergeant. Now he had donuts! Cool. This would look good on my recommendation from Vacaville to Butte County as to how I should ultimately be sentenced. Plus, I would be able to safely (hopefully) pass some time. I mean, my boss was packing heat.

I made my way down the moderately active hallway, which was approximately two hundred yards long. The corridor was about fifty feet wide. It was like being a hall monitor in grade school. With a pass, you were allowed outside the classroom—a bit of freedom. I reported all chipper and fresh, but was greeted with little fanfare—especially from the prisoner sitting in front of me, the first guy to get the sports page from the cop. He had little regard for me. He was in here for life, for murder. I was (I hoped) just passing through, although he told me repeatedly (while tossing his head back and cackling) that "You'll be back" I shuddered at the thought. I was a short-timer. A short short-timer.

I got the drill as to what was to be expected of me: just doing what I was told. Carrying messages throughout the prison was my favorite. I got to roam about freely. The lecture about my duties was similar to any first day on the job, except here, your supervisor wore a side piece and your coworker was never going home.

I saw a lot of very strange things while I traveled about the prison. Mostly, right then I wanted to see that green *San Francisco Chronicle* sports page that was *slowly* (I mean, he had all the time in the world, I guess) being read by my murderous coworker. He knew I coveted it. He was not giving an inch as he oohed and aahed over the articles. The trick from now on was to feign indifference for what he possessed. I was sure I could soon become worker of the month.

So I sat. And waited. This game had me at a distinct disadvantage against my adversary, who was well practiced at killing jail time (not to mention, people). The officer noticed the tension. Or maybe it wasn't that big a deal for this place, or at all. I mean, minor, petty work relationships (even life-threatening ones) were probably fairly common here. Maybe that's why there had been an immediate job opening. Hmmm. *How did the position open up?* I wondered as I delivered a few messages.

Just think about it. This is how archaic the communications system was. I was hand-delivering paper slips with handwritten messages to cellblocks throughout the prison. Do you think there might've been slip-ups with this system? No computers. No closed-circuit security cameras. No instant communications other than a rotary phone. I do remember looking at the one phone on our area's command center and briefly wanting to make an outside phone call, but it wasn't an all-consuming feeling. I don't think I talked on a phone (except in the visitors' area) for the entire five months. No texting for sure. No Instagram. No one was sitting around obsessing over screens.

During one of my runs, navigating the long hallways and corridors, I was sent into the restricted (for my type of imprisonment) blue side of the prison; I had been on the green side. Its name was cleverly coined from the observation that all the prisoners in my area were assigned green clothing; you can guess the coloring of the clothing on the blue side.

My first foray into the forbidden blue side, where prisoners could spend the rest of their brutal lives, was eye opening. Being on this side was extremely dangerous. Guys had little to lose. What's another murder charge when you're already sentenced to live the rest of your days locked up? There's not a lot of motivation to behave.

The "blue side" of Vacaville was where the state-of-the-art prison medical facility operated. As I traveled through it, I was once again struck with the visual of what seemed to be a Bob Mackie fashion runway show. Parading up and down the hallway were inmates who were very dolled up: long hair, makeup, polished nails, and breasts (undergoing hormonal treatment to enhance their size) held in place by bras. They were dressed to kill—literally, I suppose, in some cases. Guys were hooting and hollering. It was like a Bob Hope USO tour where he brought Ann-Margret and *Playboy* bunnies to visit the boys in Vietnam.

This was quite a spectacle to me. Even though I grew up in and around liberal San Francisco, I guess I was still pretty sheltered. I had yet to witness this type of stuff. I found it quite festive and entertaining.

Upon my return from the festivities of the blue side, on my chair was the sports page. I don't know how it got there, but I thanked everyone in the room profusely and pored over the previous night's stats. If I had only listened to my math teachers (or any teachers) with as much interest as I had when deciphering Willie Mays's lifetime batting average over the past fifteen years, I'd have been at Yale School of Medicine instead of this California Medical Facility.

Chapter 27: Don't Stand So Close to Me

"Hey. These guys are from your county!" announced my officer/ boss. He had noticed that incoming inmates were arriving from Butte County. It was weird for that place to be thought of as "mine"; I had only lived there for a few months, and most of them were horrible. I'm an Oakland native for life.

I really didn't have anybody I was expecting to know from Butte County, but I looked toward the intake area anyway and saw Bob! I started to wave, but he turned away quickly. *Oh, shit.* I thought. *Now I remember.*

I'm glad he didn't acknowledge me. Now obviously, I'm not the smartest drug dealer around—that's proven by the fact that I was sitting in this place. But even I should have known not to buddy up to a guy *entering* jail with drugs up his butt. Plus, Bob didn't really know who I was. My story was pretty suspect, and here I was a couple of days later sitting right next to the cops. I could be a big-time snitch. I watched intently but tried not to arouse any undue suspicion. The searches of the incoming prisoners seemed to be proceeding rather ordinarily (if you count several men squatting naked a few yards away with their ass cheeks spread like the Grand Canyon as ordinary). I was petrified that the look on my face was screaming out that something was amiss. I am a horrible poker player, my invites to play as numerous as the losses I have compiled.

Holding my breath, I paced for a few moments, then left the area. If something in there was actually bothering you (which was pretty much everything all the time) and someone actually inquired as to your well-being (which was never), you at least had the perfect environment to shrug them off.

Well, now, of course, our kindly sergeant (he of the *SF Chronicle* and sometimes donuts and always handgun) asked me what was bothering me. Shit. I had to immediately choose the James Dean *Rebel Without a Cause* loner attitude for this one nice guy and clam up. He shrugged at my shrugging. As Bob's search continued in the next room, I kept up the silent act—this from a guy who couldn't stop nervously chattering most all the time.

"Maybe it was his boyfriend," chimed in my murderous coworker. They started laughing.

"No, I don't know anyone," I mumbled, and kept my head down in that paper for the next thirty minutes.

Finally, Bob was processed past us. I saw his nearly waist-length ponytail go by our bulletproof windows and sighed a breath of relief. Either he had a big blow-out in one of those Butte County toilets the night before he left, or he was gonna have a bigger blowout when he got to his cell.

I saw Bob only once after that day. As I said, I kept mostly low-key. There were several cellblocks and several thousand prisoners locked in them. It wasn't exactly a feel-good environment where we were encouraged to go forth and meet and greet our fellow inmates. This wasn't the place for a Dale Carnegie seminar. Don't ask, don't tell. Don't go looking for anything unless you are looking for trouble.

My shift finished, I went back to the drudgery of the common cell area. Meals. Counts. Board games. To me they were "bored" games, interspersed with occasional terror if there had been a dispute. I just waited until I could go up to my solitary cell. When I was away from everyone (save for the flashlights shining in my face every fifteen minutes), I could mentally replenish myself. I could tick off another day of this ridiculousness. I could write and read and pretend I was somewhere else.

I finally made my way upstairs after another long, exhausting day. It's tiring to be on extreme alert every second of your existence, but that is required to continue to exist. Lionel had been moved to another section of the prison. Terry was still next door to me. We bid each other goodnight and went inside our side-by-side chambers. We were separated only by six feet of solid concrete. *If they would only put 5 percent of the costs of building prisons (and monitoring and housing, while providing food, health care, legal assistance, and recreation) into public education,* I thought, *we might not need as many prisons.* But that is a different book.

My days pretty much settled into a dull routine. At first I had to act unsurprised at the lunacy present at all moments wherever I looked. But a few weeks in, it was just another boring, wasteful, useless, petrifying day to me.

Chapter 28: Walk This Way

For instance, today I was walking out to the yard and fell into step with a Black dude. He was smaller than Lionel, but I mean, who wasn't? I struck up a conversation—nothing remarkable or memorable, nothing I hadn't done hundreds of times in multicultural Oakland where I had grown up. As I happened upon Terry and a few of his running mates, I bid my walking mate goodbye.

"What are you doing?" Terry asked. It was clear that he was the leader of this little posse.

"Nothing," came my safe reply.

"You can't talk to that nigger," Terry spat out.

"What? Why?" I asked, feeling slapped in the face by that word. I thought the Black dude was actually going to slap my face too. But he moved on.

Terry told me that I couldn't talk to anyone other than those of my own color. If I looked around, he said, I'd notice that the races all hung only with each other. I had not taken notice of this previously, but sure enough. There it was: Blacks only sitting with Blacks, Hispanics likewise, as well as whites. Not so many Asians. And here we were, firmly in the Whites Only section. Lucky there wasn't a Jews Only section. I didn't meet many during my visit here. Maybe we could have hung with the Asians. Hell, couldn't we all just get along?

This blew my mind. Knowing nothing and rapidly learning less each day, I agreed to join my new "gang." We consisted of about eight guys, none of whom amounted to much. We were the template for the wonderful Groucho Marx quote, "I wouldn't want to be in a club that would have me as a member." We were small. We weren't brilliant. Our only apparent qualifying factor was the color of our skin.

Terry laid our gang's creed down. We were to watch each other's backs. Special attention was given to me because I was lost in here. This was all agreed upon. In our semicircle was one overweight, baby-faced member. His IQ had to be no more than 80, which was about how many extra pounds (none of them muscle) he carried. He pledged his fealty the loudest. So there it was: I had protection. Even though it felt like a ten year-old condom with several leaks in it.

A few hours later, we were called in to dinner. As I made my way toward the line and got my tray, I forgot our gang's sacred number-one rule: I got separated from the rest. When I made it to a table, sitting to my right was a rough-looking (weren't they all?) Hispanic guy around forty years old. I didn't think it was his first stint in Vacaville. On my left was a guy who was the spitting image of Muhammad Ali circa 1965. He had the requisite cockiness to go along with then–Cassius Clay. Now *this* guy, I knew.

In order for this to make sense, we'll have to rewind a little. Let me go back a bit . . .

Chapter 29: Taxman

I'd been here one week now. Leaving dinner, I went across the hall to sit as far away from everyone as possible while waiting for the silverware to be counted. I noticed a bustling of activity at the far wall—this was out of the sight of the guards, as there were none in this room and no security cameras to observe us. There was a line of about thirty guys waiting to use the bathroom. This was unusual. They were all jostling and had big smiles on their faces. The man orchestrating this group activity looked exactly like young, beautiful 1960 Olympic Gold Medal winner Cassius Clay (pre–Muhammad Ali). I'd noticed this guy before. He was the obvious ringleader of this particular portion of the circus, clearly in his element, with a broad smile across his face. It was like a latter-day Clay/Ali press conference. I stayed away. It's wise to stay away from anything and everything out of the ordinary, and I didn't want to be the Howard Cosell version of this.

I watched the line slowly move along. One guy would come out of the single-person bathroom (almost as small as an airplane lavatory); another would quickly take his place inside. The guys coming out of the bathroom would sport huge smiles, giggling for the crowd and nodding appreciatively to the ringleader. It was like a kissing booth or the lobby of a Reno whorehouse (at least based on what I've heard and the pictures I've seen). Lots of teenage-boy testosterone-fueled laughing. It didn't take long to figure out what was going on.

Cassius/Ali had recruited someone to service all his new (and old) friends. This would be his calling card, an introduction to his sentence at Vacaville. The other guy? I don't know. Maybe it was his way of surviving the day. As one guy would exit the bathroom with a shit-eating grin across his face, the line would move forward one man. This continued for the next forty-five minutes, until we were given the "all clear" and allowed back into the dining area for the after-dinner games and conflicting radio station wars.

I was in no hurry to move from one room to the next, so I sat and waited as most of the guys left this area. After a few minutes, a guy left the bathroom. He was a sweet-looking man, He looked like a six-foot-tall version of Prince. He was quite effeminate, and had no shame about it. When he saw me watching, he just gave me a mournful shrug as if to say, *That's my way of getting through this here, honey.* Then he strutted out with his head held high with as much pride as he could. Everyone and everything sucked here.

He had been pimped out by the Ali character. He had performed oral sex for a few dozen guys that first night. This was their deal.

Chapter 30: American Idiot

Now the Ali lookalike was sitting to my immediate left. The tables were small and only sat four men to each one. But, lo and behold, across from me was one of my boys! My homie. My fellow gangbanger. He must've scouted me and rushed to cover me. He was the 80/80 guy (80 pounds overweight, 80 IQ), but nonetheless, my first gangbanger.

We all ate in silence, mostly ignoring each other. This seemed to be the way these meals took place. Here we all were in a crowded dining hall, and you could hear the conversation (if there was any) ten tables away.

When we were almost done, the Hispanic guy pushed his food away and hissed, "There's something missing."

I'm generally used to replying (ever so politely) when my dining companion initiates conversation, so I said, "Yeah, man. Your lady."

He looked at me like I'd just told him to go fuck the Virgin Mary. I immediately gathered that I'd stepped over a line, made another grievous faux pas. I hadn't meant anything derogatory or smart (no danger there)—I was just attempting to empathize with him (my first mistake).

I quickly interjected, "You know. Our ladies. Like, I'm missing mine, I mean." I vainly tried to right this rapidly listing ship, but I was taking on water.

He gave me a look and turned to Ali. Then he seethed back at me, "What the fuck do you know?"

I felt my slot machine of a brain spinning rapidly for a hopeful landing on a jackpot of an answer. "Man, I didn't mean anything. I just miss my lady. That's all. Sorry."

Hoo boy. *Sorry* was a complicated word around here. It could lead to a whole slew of people taking advantage of your weakness.

Things were tense, but my immediate backing down seemed to ease the situation. A few seconds slowly passed. Dinner was almost over. This would all go away soon, I hoped.

Just then, the "Champ" gave a cursory glance toward the closest dinner guard (a 250-pound man of iron) and dramatically leaned toward me, practically into my face. Since he was so tall and gangly, he could almost be in my chair. He hissed out, "Give me your roll."

Another spin of my internal slot machine went off. As I waited for the columns to stop, I wondered which roll he was talking about. I had a freshly baked roll still on my tray, and I had a fresh flesh roll that had only just been sat on. This was the same guy who had pimped out a guy from his cellblock only two weeks earlier. It was clearly a "What do I fucking do now?" moment and an "I'd better do it right too!" time. But wait! I had my homie right across from me. Granted, the weakest link in the chain (save for me), but he had my back, right?

80/80 had been our most vocal guy. The most ardent about us protecting one another! I was part of a gang now. This was what we did. I'd ask him, but I didn't know his name, nor did I know if he would understand such a complicated question. I looked across to my brother—a very different one than the one who'd sit across from me at the dinner table back home, who secretly kicked me in the shins with lethal accuracy and B-2 bomber stealth every night, but a brother nonetheless. A baby-faced brother at that. Now there was a promise of a grave threat and great bodily harm in my immediate future, much worse than what my real brother had ever perpetrated upon me. Mind you, prison Ali's hand was millimeters from my tray. Yes, the *Titanic* had hit an iceberg, but the ship could not go down!

The perceived slight I had blurted out to the Mexican Mafia leader (as I thought of him in my head now) had Ali pulling a rope-a-dope on me. He looked over at the guard, who looked like Dwayne "The Rock" Johnson (I think he must've been his father); for a brief moment, I felt relief, but then I saw that the guard's attention had been diverted to other dangerous felons. Hope plummeting, I imagined that they would be able to finish the dinner fork count with the one that was soon to be lodged in my throat.

I looked straight over at my new friend across the table. I didn't know what to expect, but what I saw was a distinct lowering of his eyes. There must've been something of great interest in his lap. Okay, I had only myself here. Looked like I had to get myself out. To be honest, my first instinct was to run and hide behind the guard like I was at home and he was my mommy's apron, but I didn't think that should be option number one. I had to do something, and it had to be the right thing, or that roll was not gonna be the last thing I would be giving up nightly.

So I slowly picked up my soft, buttery roll. I placed it delicately between my middle "fuck you" finger and my thumb. Hey, if I was going to die soon, I was at least going down with a "fuck you" to all these fuckers.

I looked over at my hungry friend and announced, "I'm gonna eat my roll." And with that, I took a pronounced (perhaps my last ever) bite. I must say, that roll tasted great.

He stared at me hatefully and gave another look to the Cartel Lord, then to the Rock's daddy. And then—he made like I wasn't worth the trouble. Which, of course, I wholeheartedly agreed with! No other words would be necessary—luckily for me, because I almost choked, my throat was so dry.

Incident over. I promise you, he has never given it another thought these past forty years. Me? It took as much out of me as if I had gone eight rounds with the real Ali. I needed a new gang. Or no gang. Or a good gang. Or to get the gang out of there.

Chapter 31: The Letter

Another day, another dollar. Well, in this case, no dollar. In my prison job, I made three cents an hour. My big fantasy of pulling down big prison bucks was just that. Hey, I would've done it for free—at least I got to read my newspaper. This was back in the day when the paper was king. I think it cost ten cents daily then. The incomparable Herb Caen kept me aware that there was a real world out there. I remember one of his columns, when he wrote how the sounds of San Franciscans celebrating on a warm summer eve in the forties and fifties traveled over the Bay to Alcatraz. It drove the inmates mad. Now I understood.

Nothing was particularly out of the ordinary this day. Unless you count that I was living among thousands of violent criminals under constant lock and key, being monitored twenty-four hours a day, suppressed in a carefully crafted and honed manner that had been professionally perfected over hundreds of years.

I'm not going to get into the politics or economics of why we imprison so many (mostly poor people and people of color) in our society. I am certainly no expert. I do think there needs to be a place where people who are dangerous to the general population should be sequestered. But obviously, someone had figured out how to make a lot of money through this process. Some of us (my hand is raised) need not be punished in this fashion. From my now-expert point of view, I believe some crimes should be punished by allowing the perpetrators to do beneficial labor (hand raised again) for the area that they committed their crimes. Manual labor. Safely away from the general population.

As I said before, I also believe there are many people in prison who should never be released. I shudder to think of them now and wonder if any are free and near my family. They are dangerous. Again, I don't know the solution.

I safely ate a meal, then headed to the TV room to wait for the silverware/lethal weapon check. Might I add here that while the TV was on, the sound wasn't? Sometimes it was tuned into the news, but this was way before the twenty-four-hour news cycle of today. There were no streaming chyrons scrolling across the top and the bottom of the screen. Breaking news was rare. If there was any, it probably involved some of these guys' friends. There weren't such things as televised car chases—mostly weather, sports, and a few local stories of interest, escaped cattle and the like. We were in the boondocks, after all.

Most time spent was wasted time. I got that it was a punishment, but I wish there had been something constructive that someone better and smarter than I could figure out to do with all this wasted time. Plus, my God, the resources that were being squandered. I read in a 2018 paper (forty years later) that since 1978, there have been twenty-two prisons built in California, and exactly *one* university. I didn't ever graduate from any of those universities. Again, I am not capable of solving this issue. I'm just here to observe, recollect, and recount my little tale.

The days and nights were excruciatingly boring. Of course, they were speckled with abject fear, but for the most part, I engaged in watching the black mold inside my cell reproduce. (No, seriously—I actually found myself doing this one evening, but it was time consuming, and I found no results.)

I read. I read for hours every day. Like I said before, when I was reading, it didn't matter where I was. I was all-focused on words.

One day, while I was engrossed in a book, a guy approached me. He was white, so I guessed it was okay for us to talk. He was writing a letter to his girlfriend. I guess the word had gotten out that I could write. I mean, like literally. Just put letters in the correct place behind one another. He asked if I would help him say the right things. This seemed harmless enough. We made a time for the next day. The location was easy enough to figure out.

Chapter 32: Dazed and Confused

April 29, 1978. The next day.

And this, my friend, is how easily trouble can begin.

I was out in the yard enjoying my solitude and my latest escapist novel, along with my fantasy that I was in Bali, when my new friend/client showed up. I had kind of forgotten about our planned meeting. This was something I should not have done—you did *not* abandon an obligation to anyone in here. It was difficult to avoid the confrontation.

So here he was. I looked up and, with his face in full sunlight, I could see a lot of deep wounds, external and internal. What did I expect? This is what I mean by everyone in here being unlike the people you'd normally interact with in your day-to-day out there. First, I noticed the tic: his body would involuntarily jolt every twenty seconds or so. He looked like an absent-minded professor; his glasses sat misaligned on his nose and were held together by thick tape. He had shoulder-length, stringy, oily brown hair; his scraggly beard was flecked with food, and for some reason he had tiny bits of (unused, I hoped) toilet paper in there as well. He was clutching a nearly three-inch-thick binder crammed with papers that were falling out on all sides. I could see his scribbles and crossed-out writing.

Uh oh, I thought.

"Here's some of what I've got so far," he stuttered as he clumsily clambered down, sitting close beside me, completely invading my personal space. He thrust his tome to me. Think Unabomber Manifesto times three here. I slowly opened to a page, and it practically disintegrated in my fingers.

This was worse and crazier than I had imagined. The writing was indecipherable. I estimated that it might've been longer than 300 pages written in microscopic block lettering. I had clearly put myself in a bind with this man's binder. I began to read, but it was more like deciphering cave drawings. Unintelligible ones.

Within thirty seconds, he asked me, "What do you think?"

I exhaled, said, "I gotta have a moment here," and frantically searched for anything on the page that I could grasp onto.

I'll admit, I was up against it there. I read and I mumbled and I nodded, and I got nothing. I was buying time, but there was nothing but this going on around me.

I looked over at him and got hit with a waft of bad breath and putrid body odor, but I also saw the ache. Now a tear running down one of the crevices on his face. I felt the desperate pain. *That* I could understand. Maybe we could use some of this. I was beginning to suss out an age-old story.

Still, I had barely gotten past the first paragraph, and that was only so I could pretend that I actually understood any of what I had read. After a few more moments gathering facts and beginning to formulate an approach, I took a deep breath through my mouth and resorted to verbal communication without inhaling.

I grasped an inkling of the situation. Mostly (I surmised) it was a tale of undying love. "Couldn't live without you," etc. Basic poems and love songs from the beginning of time. Al Green, Sinatra, the Beatles. Unlike Lennon/McCartney, I must admit there were more than a few "I will slice your face up like a melon if you fuck me over" passages, which I gently suggested might not be the best to include in the general undying-love theme. *Aha. Knife wounds on his face! That's what those strange marks were. I'm so stupid.*

"I don't know. How about, 'If you don't love me, I'll die'?" I offered. In his case, it was more like, "If you don't love me, I'll kill." The dying was the only consistent piece.

Just then, Terry approached, asking what was going on. When I told him, he asked my friend to give us a second. Thinking we may steal them, my pal would not leave without his scriptures; once he had them (which was a huge load off my lap), he wandered a few feet away.

Then Terry turned and asked accusingly, "What the fuck are you doing?"

It seemed as if he were always asking me that. Of course, it was a rhetorical question at that point.

"You do *not* want to get involved in these crazy fuckers' lives!"

Now this, I understood.

"But . . ." I stammered.

"*No fucking buts!*" he cut me off.

I reminded Terry that the unwritten yet fiercely adhered-to prison rules were that I had agreed to assist, so I had to provide my part of the equation or face great consequences.

Looking to make sure the guy was out of earshot, Terry lit into me. "Do you even know who this guy wants you to write to?" Of course, I did not.

It appeared that the desperate love letter from our guy on the "green side" was to his former lover, who was now the possession of another convict on the "blue side." These relationships were territorial and violent; they could become brutal, vicious, and heartbreaking to witness. When I was on the blue side a few days earlier, what I had thought was just a harmless viewing was actually like parading show horses before the race, with the biggest, baddest bidder claiming what they want. This often led to bloodshed.

Fortunately, I never witnessed any of this in person, but I heard the threats and saw tears being shed, just like minutes before in front of me. My client's boyfriend was now gone, the "property" of another man; the new man held all "rights" to his new property, until his in turn were challenged. This could be deadly. The property could also be voluntarily replaced for another, if a younger, newer, or fresher man came along. If you were dumped and not chosen by another quickly, your protection was ended. Often the new partner was given a gift of loyalty—this came in the form of having their former lover disfigured, to prove allegiance and eliminate the threat of his return.

So. Harmless laughs? I think not. This was when I stopped shaving and showering. I wasn't a pretty boy (even though Gustine thought so), and I didn't want anyone to think differently.

Terry and I brought Shakespeare back; then, together (with Terry closely monitoring everything), we continued working. I guess we had helped. Our customer seemed thrilled as he went off to send his letter, certain that the words would solve all the issues the relationship would have to hurdle. I could also relate to that. I felt each letter that I wrote to Amber would fix everything. I figured it would at least make us stronger together.

I turned to Terry and said, "Now that wasn't so bad, was it?"

Glowering at me, he barked, "It will be fine as long as her current boyfriend doesn't find a way to find us and fuck us up for helping our friend out!"

Only then did I learn that the girl of our guy's dreams was actually the new property of a 6′5″ muscle-loaded lifer living on the blue side, right next to us! Try to couch that image into "If I Fell" by the Beatles.

I really was out of my element. Sigh. Back to dinner. Count. Boredom. Upstairs to read and cross off another day.

Chapter 33: Please Mr. Postman

By now, word of my imprisonment had gone out to my friends, and I was getting letters every day. I was certain I was such a low risk that opening my mail was a mere formality. I loved getting these letters. I still do. Too bad today no one writes anymore. There would normally be one from my dad. His were always supportive and encouraging.

I wrote back to everyone who wrote me a letter. I wrote Amber long letters which retrospectively weren't much different from the letter I had helped write for my also-obsessed friend (save for the threats of harm). Granted, it was only similar because she was also incarcerated; I hoped the similarities ended there.

Today at lunch, I was sitting with a few guys. I mean, what else is new? There was a lot of time sitting around and a lot of guys to sit around with. As usual, the conversation turned to the crimes that each guy had committed, the ones that had led them to their current audience.

It began with the lurid description of the crime, and always included the litany of errors that had befallen the victim. By "victim," they meant themselves. It had always been someone else's fault. There were lots of knowing nods and appreciative "mm-hms" from the listeners that reminded me of a gospel church revival service; these were my cues as to which ways I had better respond. Each story included elaborate schemes (including lots of planning time) to make sure the storytellers eliminated their mistakes next time. These ranged from simple alterations to the crime to simply killing all the witnesses.

These were very difficult conversations for me. You see, I had no plans to continue with the behavior that had landed me here, and I fully accepted that I was the cause of my own residency. When the murderous lifer inmate at my job was hoarding the newspaper, he used to say to me, "You will be back here soon." Then he would throw his head back and wickedly cackle. This would really freak me out and upset me greatly, which, of course, was his intention. "Shit downhill on everyone" was the philosophy.

Most everyone says they will never be back. But what most everyone also says is that the *reason* they won't be back is that they will perfect their crime. This floored me. This place wasn't about rehabilitation—it was an academy in becoming a better criminal.

This is why I believe this prison system is greatly flawed. It is not a deterrent. I reiterate, I do not know how to solve this situation. But I also (having first-hand experience) believe that letting many (if not most) of these guys out at all is letting gravely dangerous people loose on innocent and unsuspecting future victims.

Let's just say that 99 percent (perhaps more) of the conversations in prison are about crime. Crimes committed; crimes gotten away with; crimes to be committed more successfully in the future. The latter was the most common. Mind you, the conversation rarely (in fact, never that I can recall) ventured into the area of *not* revisiting the scenes of the crime. It mostly (if not always) included lengthy oral dissemination of strategies toward perfecting the crime that had landed them in prison. When this led to the unanimous verdict of eliminating all the "loose ends" ("human beings"), I could barely believe my ears. I still held onto guilt and remorse from not RSVP-ing to Nancy Taylor's sweet birthday invitation back in sixth grade.

These guys were not only unrepentant, but deeply angry at having been caught for committing their heinous crimes. "I'm gonna kill that bitch next time" was followed by a chorus of "Mm-hmm. You got to." Though I gulped and my jaw fell further, I managed to remain silent as

I had been advised; I even nodded my head at the appropriate moments and "mm-hmm-ed" at what I surmised were the right times.

Finally, late in the afternoon, after hours of these conversations had droned on, I'd had enough. Snapping awake from my non-reverie, I queried, "Um, has anyone ever thought of maybe, perhaps"—dramatic pause and throat-clearing for effect here—"*not* going back and re-entering the cycle of crime and inevitable punishment?"

I looked around the circle of hardened men, then quickly back at my feet. I hadn't yet been punched, so I continued. Tentatively. "I mean, let's not even take into account the vast amounts of damage done psychologically, physically, and financially to the victims and their loved ones."

I tried to couch this in as light-hearted a way as possible, all the while recognizing my audience. I played *to* them, never down. I was quite serious. My questioning was honest. I spoke softly and chose my words carefully, attempting to instill some logic in my speech. I even quoted that old song: "I fought the law and the law won."

After I'd spoken for about ten minutes (which seemed like ten hours), there followed a period of silence, which also seemed like ten hours. The silence was not because some collective enlightenment had just transformed them. It was more like collective bewilderment. This message did not resonate with anyone. As I looked up at each confused face, it seemed as if I had been speaking Swahili. A couple of them laughed nervously, as if they thought I had been joking. I wasn't. I was sad.

But there it was. I had said my piece. I had tried my hand at rehabilitating a few people, and it had fallen on deaf ears.

This would be the last time I suggested anything as outlandish as this to any other inmate, except for another young kid once several months later. He had brains and charisma; he looked like a young Axl Rose. He was already so immersed in the criminal lifestyle that I'm afraid I again had little effect. He loved the song "Baker Street" by

Gerry Rafferty. It played a lot that summer. He would close his eyes and transcend to his happy place. I have to believe he's dead or in a not-so-happy place right now. I hope I'm wrong.

Chapter 34: Take This Job and Shove It

I thought it was high time I got another job. I may have reached my glass (in this case, tons of cement) ceiling. My coworker convict was liking me less and less, and my boss, with his handcuffs and handgun, was eyeing me for a promotion to a long-term position. These two had been together for years, and potentially had many more to go—one was in here for life without parole for first-degree murder, and the other was some fifteen or twenty years from retirement. That was the equivalent of five to seven years in prison (if you spend one-third of your life at work) for the sergeant. I wanted to remove myself from the potentially deadly workplace politics. It was becoming a frustrating daily head game to finally get the sports page passed down to me. On top of that, the brush with Manson and his heavily armed goons had tempered my enthusiasm for my short career as a telegram message delivery boy. It was time to move on.

Chapter 35: Message In a Bottle

May 11, 1978. The next day.

I received a message myself! It was handed to me by the guy I'd first witnessed coming out of the bathroom after he had given blow jobs to several dozen of our finest inmates, who introduced himself to me as Reggie. He had since become the secretary of the cellblock. He would sit primly at his small, carefully organized metal desk and inform all of us of our upcoming appointments. He was very sweet, like our own den mother, even if his den was this horrid pack of wolves.

My message said that I was to meet with my psychologist the next morning! Finally! This was the first of the two required meetings needed to evaluate me and send the recommendation for sentencing back to Butte County. *Let's get this show on the road and end this charade.*

I cradled my paper slip and stared at it all night. I could hardly sleep. This was to be one of the most important interviews of my life. I did not want to mess it up. I really didn't want to run into a guy like the probation officer in Butte County. With him, it hadn't mattered what I said, because he was predisposed to lock me up.

Before I went up to bed, I asked other guys what might be the preferred approach to impress my shrink, but from the quizzical looks I received I gathered that this was going to be one of those rare times my own instincts would serve me best here. My cellblock secretary friend Reggie was the most helpful. We talked a lot. He was intelligent and empathetic. He also had experience with the way things worked around this place. He assured me that I would excel in my interview and offered again to calm my nerves and comfort me behind the bookcase, but I kept a careful physical distance from him. He was always friendly and flirtatious, but I needed to stay focused on the goal of getting out as soon as possible—and in one piece.

The night slogged on. I had five letters delivered to me at 3:00 a.m. and read them over and over. I couldn't wait until I could be face to face with the letter writers. As usual, there was an encouraging letter from my dad. He was like a coach motivating a player who had just wandered off course a little. Or in this case, a lot.

Chapter 36: Nothing Else Matters

Okay. Breakfast had been safely consumed. Three hours until my meeting. Try sitting or standing around with no TV, phone, newspaper, car, coffee, girlfriend, any friend, or anything else to kill the time. You cannot even nap some of the time away. Too scary and also forbidden. It's rough.

Finally! My time had arrived. I made it to my appointed destination—no Manson sightings on the way. So much was at stake for me; so much was riding on what was about to occur behind this door.

"I got this!" I said to myself. Even though every encounter with the legal system for the past six months had been met with disaster, I remained optimistic. Or stupid, I guess.

I took a deep breath, then gently knocked on the door.

"Come in," I heard from the other side. It sounded like a friendly voice.

I entered a small, sparsely decorated office. It was mostly dominated by a desk piled three feet high with paper-filled folders. There was, of course, no computer monitor on the desk, but a typewriter. A manual one at that. It seemed like I could've been meeting with one of my college professors during office hours—that is, I imagined that was the case. I had never made those office-hour appointments on the outside.

Looking the psychologist in the eye, I shook his hand graciously. I was polite and ever so respectful, basically being myself. Of course, I was extremely nervous. I was sitting across from a man who was very experienced in dealing with men who posed huge, problematic possibilities. I was hoping not to join that group. I wanted to be a blip on this man's office radar.

He seemed curious and a little open to this agreeable young man presently sitting across the desk from him—wary, of course, but how many cons must have been attempted by the legions who had sat there before me? And I must admit, when you're imprisoned and punished by society, you begin to question not just the sanity of said society, but your own reality. *Do I really belong here? Am I crazy? Is all this an illusion in my head? Have I actually been locked up for years? Am I a menace to myself and others so much that I need to be locked away from people? I mean, am I really going to be in here for years to come? Is Charles Manson the type of person I should forever be associated with from now on? Am I actually Charles Manson?* The mind wanders.

We exchanged introductory dialogue. It was nice to swap a couple of sentences with another person without a description of a horrific crime dominating the conversation. I was sure I was being measured, monitored, and analyzed, but I did not care. My story was pretty innocuous, as far as I could tell. Let's just say I had not heard of a petty crime that came close to the one that put me there. Still, I was still petrified by memories of Gustine, by the possibility that this could backfire into another one of those situations. I prayed (well, not literally) that this person was not in touch with that bastard back in Butte County.

When a natural lull in the conversation occurred, he opened the file on me that sat in front of him. I saw his eyes quickly scan down the first page, then the next. Then he closed the file and looked up at me. I waited patiently for the other shoe to drop. And then it did.

"Jesus Christ!" he bellowed.

Oh, boy, I thought. *Now I am really fucked.*

Then he slammed his open palm on the report that he had been reading. I froze. "Fucking Butte County! They think it's okay to send you here to teach you a lesson? This is insane. You are in danger here. This is a mistake."

At first, I could only blink. I swallowed, but found my throat was constricted. I almost leapt up and hugged him. "That's what I've been saying!" I managed.

"You've got to shut your mouth and stay away from everyone and anything until this stupid ordeal is over."

"Yes! Yes!" I answered. "Can I stay in this office until it's over?" I added, and "Can you make it over tomorrow?" Unfortunately, the wheels of justice did not move as rapidly as I would've wished—this was before real criminals like Donald Trump were pardoning friends of Kim Kardashian en masse.

My new best friend flipped through my accordion file folder (apparently it was the first time he had read it) and tsk-tsked at me for being sent to state prison for selling a quarter gram of cocaine—a lesser quantity than the sugar you put (or used to put) on your cereal in the morning. He restated that they were "fools" up in Butte County, which I certainly wasn't about to argue with. He said he would send along a favorable review, one that would hopefully be followed as the judge in Butte County had promised—and my freedom would follow that.

We talked for a few more minutes. Heck, I had all day, and I did not want to leave this place or this nice man. Can I say, that "I loved him?" He emphatically repeated how ludicrous this was and how I should avoid all interaction with the rest of the general population. Then he hesitated. I was afraid he was going to burst out into a heinous chortle and tell me he was just joking, so I inquired fearfully as to what was on his mind. He said he had just had a thought, but it might not be such a great idea. I had liked all his ideas so far, so I was all ears. "Please elaborate," I said.

He told me that on review of my report, it showed a very high IQ, one of the highest that he had come in contact with. Considering the surrounding candidates, I was not particularly surprised. Tactfully, let's just say the bar was low. I knew I had a high IQ—not much common sense, though. In parent/teacher meetings, I had always heard, "So much potential. So much of it wasted on frivolity." I did test well, though, I supposed.

The psychologist asked if, contrary to his earlier recommendation, I would be interested in actually administering the IQ exams to the incoming inmates. I would be doing this in an area just down the hall from him, and he virtually assured my safety. Well, he added, I'd be as safe as most any place in here, which was not extremely safe at all. I now wanted to find a cot and sleep here. Or maybe just under his desk at night.

I'd had my fill of running around the prison delivering messages. Even though it was fascinating at times, it really could be quite dangerous. Any time you were doing something out of the norm, you were a target, and there was always the risk of having a shotgun leveled at you when Charlie Manson or any of his buddies strolled past. Besides, things at the front office were becoming a huge drag. The San Francisco Giants were tanking earlier than usual, so the ordeal of getting to the sports page wasn't even worth all the extra effort. I agreed to the new position. It was easy to quit. I just didn't show up. What were they going to do? Arrest me?

I traded my sports page for test booklets, the only summer in my entire life I did not read about baseball first thing each day. My new job description was simple, or so I thought. Just explain the rules of the test-taking and clear out for the next two hours. I thought I could do this!

Yet how many teachers had I disrupted, annoyed, outright tortured, and treated ever so disrespectfully over the years? Little did I know about the dedication and extremely hard work that a teacher puts in. Boy, karma really is a bitch.

Chapter 37: "School's Out" for Summer

Okay, here's the deal. I would administer two to ten tests to the incoming prisoners each day. Business was booming! At first, I would carefully explain the rules and quietly retreat to the back of the room. I tried to be kind, and *never* spoke down to or disrespected anyone. Still, I wasn't there to get the Teacher of the Year award. I was purely doing this to receive my "Get Out of Jail" card as soon as possible, ideally with no permanent knife scars along my throat. I didn't give two shits if they cheated. I mean, that probably would not have been the worst thing they'd done, given the location of the testing site. Plus, how do you cheat on an IQ test?

By the end of the week, things had loosened up in my classroom. I mean, I was never exactly strict, but I began to enjoy my newfound attention and power. Instead of cutting up as a student, I performed these immature antics as an instructor. I'm sure it was foolish, and I could've said (and probably did say) many things that would have gotten me beaten to within an inch of my life, but I was enjoying entertaining myself and others. It relieved some of the tedium. I must say, I had my students in stitches. I just hoped they didn't want to put *me* in them also. I made jokes at their expense, but I nurtured them too, con to con. I really wanted them to do well. So maybe we cheated a little bit? Big deal. Maybe there is a study somewhere now that shows how the IQs really spiked upward during the months of May to June 1978 in Vacaville State Prison. You're welcome.

Anyway, it made for a bit of excitement (at least for me), shaking my head in horror (sometimes mock, sometimes real) at questions posed by incoming inmates waiting to take the exam. I suppose I would have experienced even more extreme horror if I paused to think about the crimes these individuals I was calling imbeciles had committed. Honestly, who was the real imbecile here?

I'd sigh. I'd groan. I'd roll my eyes dramatically. I'd ask *"Really?"* in feigned agony. But I wanted to help, and I think my fellow caged animals sensed this. I was called "Professor" for the first (and last) time in my life.

There were no rules in my classroom. Well, one: Do not kill the teacher. How could I enforce them, anyway? I couldn't possibly ask people not to behave the way I had behaved in every classroom I had ever been in. Heck, here I was fucking off, and I was ostensibly the "professor." Goofing off was a good thing! Cheating was allowed at all times—actually, encouraged! Who really knew the right answer anyway, and who really cared? This was an alternate universe. If a guy was gonna be locked up for the next thirty years, or for the rest of his life, did it really matter if the answer was "A" or "C" on a multiple-choice exam?

When I wasn't jiving around with my students, I would write letters to my dad and my friends. Boy, if there had only been such a thing as Facebook back then, I wonder how many likes I would have gotten. "Hey look! Here's a selfie of me and your hometown murderer murdering the essay question in the IQ test." When I wrote those letters, it was like when I was reading a book: I could've been in the South Detention Wing or the South of France. When your brain is focused and occupied on a faraway subject, you are there. That is my lesson. Hey, maybe I am a professor.

Chapter 38: Walk on the Wild Side

MAY 19, 1978. A FEW DAYS LATER.

I had been in Vacaville for over a month, and I was really sick of it. I'd *been* sick of it over a month earlier. I had seen my required evaluators. I'd seen the reports they were sending back to Butte County, and they were very positive, recommending my sentence end upon my return to the Oroville courtroom. This was called a "ninety-day OP [observation period]," named for the estimated time it would take to go through the system and be evaluated. This was where they evaluated you. (Duh. Some professor I am.) At any rate, it was prison-rumored that this could also take as little as forty-five days if everything went swimmingly. I was doing my synchronized part.

I was very antsy. I completed my daily routines and just waited. It was boring. It was also claustrophobic. Each day I would watch cars passing by on nearby Highway 80, on their way to Lake Tahoe. I had heard through letters about my friends' summer plans, and I was feeling isolated. Each day I found myself getting lower and lower. It was FOMO coupled with extra fear. I was eating, but I was losing a lot of weight. I think I had come in weighing about 165 pounds, some of them from nervous eating—well, I was still nervously eating, but now weighed 145 pounds. I left prison at under 130. There's a diet you don't hear much about: the "Scare the Shit Out of You Diet." You definitely do not want to experience it.

I'd have to return to my home base cellblock about four or five times each day. Everyone had to be in their assigned cellblocks for all meals and the ensuing head (and potential weapons) counts—plus, you were to report immediately to your cellblock for any emergencies, of which there were many. I'd usually sit by myself. I was quite depressed.

Every time I returned to my accommodations, I looked hopefully at our cellblock secretary, Reggie; he always gave me an empathic and heartfelt shrug and shake of the head "no" when I asked if my transfer order back to Butte County had arrived. We had formed a little friendship, I supposed. At least we weren't enemies. Hell, for a newly minted professor, I sure didn't know much. This cycle, me approaching his desk with my hopes high only to be crushed back down, had been going on for a couple of weeks.

Finally, Reggie told me I needed to "calm myself down." When I didn't understand, he offered himself to do the calming.

I gotta tell you, outside of my interactions with Reggie, I had never been approached sexually while in prison (except back in Butte County by that vile PO officer), and I had never gotten into any other type of physical altercation. Maybe the latter was because I did genuinely outsmart those few instances where a fight may have occurred—mainly by simply feigning disinterest. Believe me, I was indeed disinterested in having my ass kicked.

But it was hard in that place. It was cold. No one was nice. Here was someone who put his hand on my shoulder and offered comfort. At that moment, it struck me: I hadn't even been touched in nearly two months. Not even by myself, as I had vowed to save it for Amber when we would finally be able to be together again. (That did not turn out as great as I planned, by the way.) So, I was tempted. It was a kind offer. He wanted to take me behind the bookcases (the emptiest spot in the prison) and perform oral sex on me. At that point, I was very vulnerable. I was thinking to myself, *Ah, what the hell?* I mean, I had witnessed and felt so many shitty things. Here was someone actually being sweet and nice.

Now mind you, in the real world out there, I would never have even considered this. Not that there's anything wrong with it—I am not homophobic, just not homosexual. But inside there, everything was topsy-turvy. And I do love blow jobs. I mean, what guy doesn't?

Still, eventually I came to a realization: I was just not interested. Maybe I wasn't in the mood. No matter how nicely it was offered, I just didn't want to. "Maybe some other time," I demurred, having heard that excuse from many girls I had asked out.

After thanking him, I went back to my lonely seat to try to speed up time. I could just imagine: Reggie had blown half the cell-block with no consequences, but I'd be caught getting a hand job behind the bookcases and be labeled a sex offender for the rest of my life. It probably would have added ten more years to my already-ridiculous sentence, and it would've been a barrel of laughs to explain to my dad. I think he was bottoming out in his tolerance of me. I could also imagine hearing all the gory details read back to me in glorious legalese back in the Oroville courtroom, spoken by my spurned probation officer. Given my current luck, I'd be the only non-convicted felon to be convicted of a felony while waiting to be convicted of a possible misdemeanor.

Let's just say Reggie and I parted as friends, and I did finally get my transfer notice from him a few weeks later. When he again asked me to go behind the bookcases for a celebration, I turned him down, but I did run into him on the outside in a very odd manner. He was one of only two people I ever saw again.

Chapter 39: Space Oddity

June 1, 1978. A few days later.

It was my ten-year bar mitzvah anniversary! Ah, I guess neither the congregation nor I could have predicted this little side trip based on the speech I had given on the *bimah* just ten short years earlier. "Rabbi, Cantor, thank you for preparing me to become a man. I will need it when I am confronted by the other angry men wanting to harm me in various and sundry ways in the Vacaville State Prison." I must have attended hundreds of bar and bat mitzvahs in my days at temple, and none of them had included those words. Maybe they did at the reform temple.

I had been imprisoned for two months. If you had asked me two months earlier whether I thought I could survive that, I'd have said it was impossible. I guess in some ways, I *had* become a man.

Still, the boredom was excruciating. My constant awareness of the monumental waste of time was mounting daily. The pressure was severe. It was frustrating to be locked in a cage. I duly administered my tests, but the novelty had run its course. Then I'd sluggishly troop out to the yard.

It was around noon that day, another warm and beautiful early summer Northern California day. I was almost tempted to lie down on the lawn, close my eyes, and relax, but I chose to lean back on my elbows and keep my eyes open. It's just not safe to let your guard down. Closing your eyes is a form of suicide. Then I saw a fairly familiar figure some fifty feet away. He was making his way toward me.

I didn't know what to do. Literally. I know it sounds crazy, but I really had no idea how to react to any situation in there. Any one of them could be harmful. I didn't want to attract any attention, and I didn't want to ignore or disrespect the rapidly approaching man. Also, it was too late to flat-out run.

"Hey, man!" said Bob.

"Wow! It's so great to see you!" I said, and found myself truly meaning it. No hugs. No shaking of hands. I mean, just as easily as he could've shaken my hand he could've shanked me. It could've been a test, or an order, or a mistake for seeing me when he arrived. Today, it was just a nod and a good feeling. Bob was on the blue side of the prison. He was hoping to stay in Vacaville for his many-years-long sentence; the alternative was to be sent to a prison such as San Quentin or another hideous place. He was doing as well as could be expected; business was booming, he told me, and he even had a bit to share with me.

I had stopped smoking pot a couple of years earlier, after it had become too strong for me. It made me paranoid. When I smoked it, I felt like my body was fragile and my bones were too brittle to hold myself up; I thought my knees would buckle and my fingers would snap. I felt my blood coursing through my heart. Yeah, it wasn't the best drug for me. But I thought to myself, *Oh, what the fuck. What could be so bad about getting high right now?* Reality sucked. Besides, it was kind of an honor when someone wanted to share something with you, especially something coveted. It was bad form (I guessed) to refuse. What could go wrong here?

Bob proudly procured the most spindly-looking joint I had ever seen. Sunlight streamed through most of the poorly wrapped paper that surrounded the miniscule amount of marijuana—we were about to smoke mostly Zig-Zag paper. That was fine with me, because I remembered which orifice the container of marijuana had traveled to prison in. The less I ingested, the better.

Doing my best not to think about inhaling things that had formerly resided inside Bob's ass, I took my first puff in years. Then I had a huge, very uncool coughing spasm. Oh yeah, I'm cool. Bob took a few hits, and then I managed to finish off the joint. I think I may have taken in two lungfuls.

We sat there. Then I realized that I was stoned—actually, I was *very* stoned. Either sprinkling the pot with butt juice increased its potency, or my tolerance was zero. I suspect the latter. I was a known lightweight. I guess the circus-like circumstance around me could have also enhanced my high; I could not say for sure. In fact, I couldn't say much at all. I was very wasted. And it was a good time! A goofy high. I was enjoying myself. The grass (on the field) looked lush and beautiful and green. The basketball players seemed poetic. Even the prison buildings and their barbed wire had a symmetrical look that, if you squinted, was reminiscent of an Escher wood carving.

It wasn't me who heard the repeated announcement over the loudspeakers first. "Hey! Isn't that you?" Bob said, sitting up.

What the fuck?! I thought. *You gotta be shitting me.* No pun intended. Then I heard it again.

"Prisoner Beren B-91593Z. Prisoner B-91593Z Beren. Report to Gate 1."

I could not believe my ears. Immediately my thoughts were that this pertained to my transfer back up to Butte County. Of course, that (plus Amber) was all I thought about, so my mind would leap there no matter what happened. But I knew this wasn't the way you received your transfer, so that was out. Then I thought that maybe, out of the hundreds of prisoners in the yard (not to mention dozens of guards with shotguns and binoculars manning the towers surrounding us), one had identified me as smoking pot and reported it.

Yeah, there was my old pot paranoia buddy back in full bloom. I thought I was headed straight to a centralized testing zone and would soon be charged with a felony and sent away forever.

"Get going!" Bob said, breaking my wildly freaked-out thoughts.

He pointed me in the right direction, and I made the long walk across the yard. I thought every eye was locked onto my back, all the sounds of basketball games, shouting, and crashing weights coming to a halt as the inmates stared.

I wondered if Bob (and the Butte County assholes) had set me up. I wondered if one of my family members was dead and this was how they were notifying me. I had never before heard another prisoner being called off the yard like this. I imagined a lot of speculation from the rest of the entire prison, whispers of "Who is this motherfucker?" rippling across the yard. I too was wondering who this motherfucker was. Ah. Welcome back, my old friend THC. I've missed thee.

When I made it to the first gate, I took a chance and glanced back at the yard—and there was absolutely no change in any person there.

After I showed my ever-present ID card and they confirmed it was me, like a VIP, I was rushed backstage. I traversed alone through several sectors, crisscrossing further into the inner sanctum of the entire prison. It was a warren of hallways and locked-off chambers. At the end of each sector, someone met me, checked me off, and pointed me off toward the next. Maybe I was gonna meet the band!

Now I was about to pass the warden's office! The actual fucking warden! Prisoner B-91593Z was about to hit the big time. The hallways were old-fashioned wood. They looked more like administrative offices in an Ivy League university (not that I had seen one, my "Professor" moniker notwithstanding). Two guards were stationed outside the warden's office. I had already been patted down five times on this walk, so they must have decided I couldn't really cause any trouble; they just pointed me down yet another nicely carpeted hallway. I had not seen carpets (nor felt them underneath my feet) in a while.

I walked around a corner, where yet another set of guards was stationed outside a door. My buzz was definitely killed by now. Two more guards were inside the room. Your taxpayer dollars were working OT here. *C'mon. Could this all be for the smoking of one skinny-ass joint? I mean, honestly, with all the other crazy shit going on all over this place and out on that yard?*

One guard opened the door wider, and I peered inside to see a comfortably furnished office. Inside it sat two distinguished-looking gentlemen. They were wearing suits and ties. One was facing away and smoking—perhaps this would hide the reek of pot I may have carried with me.

Can they test for marijuana in my bloodstream? I wondered. It was 1978. I don't know. I could probably say the words "I don't know" after every thought I had.

The room was dimly lit, far from any outside windows. As my eyes adjusted, I struggled to gaze upon its contents. My retinas enlarged as my eyeballs grew accustomed to the dim light; I was then able to absorb the image in front of me.

"*Dad!*" I shrieked, which made the other man turn in my direction.

To my shock/horror, it turned out to be his best friend, Judge Stan Golde. Normally, it would have been a pleasure to be in the presence of these two fine men, but these circumstances were far from the norm. Not only was I supremely embarrassed to see Stan, I was also petrified. To my credit, I realized immediately that this little social gathering wasn't just a terrible idea, but could become (for me) very dangerous. They didn't call me the Professor around here for nothing.

I stopped dead (no pun intended) in my tracks, well outside the entrance to the room. "Am I leaving here right now?"

My dad answered sadly, "Well, no . . . I came here to see how you're doing. And look! Stan is with me!"

That I could see. You see, Stan, who now stubbed out his ever-present cigarette, had held the gavel and meted out some very hard sentences to many of the inmates I was now sharing intimate quarters with. Not that I didn't disagree with some of his decisions (especially after spending some time with these men), but harming me would be very good payback for the many-years-to-maybe-even-a-life-sentence the guys here were looking to serve.

I purposefully did not even enter the room. Holding up my hands very high like the criminal I was, I explained loudly for all the prying ears that I would not be coming into that room. With that, I turned around and quickly left the proximity of these men.

I made sure the guards (who loved trading inside information with the prisoners) near this room were quite clear that I'd had no contact or communication with Stan Golde. My dad was only guilty of doing whatever he thought would be best for his son, but Stan should have known this would be a terrible idea. How could I go back into what was now my world and explain to my fellow inmates that this guy (or *any* judge), who had sentenced them to many years in prison (admittedly for crimes they had committed), was my daddy's fraternity brother at the Jewish frat house Alpha Epsilon Pi at UC Berkeley? How could I communicate to these guys that he had performed an *aliyah* (a reading of the Torah) at my bar mitzvah, or that he had given me a very nice desktop pen and pencil set? Mainly, though, how could I possibly communicate these thoughts while being gang-pummeled, sliced, and possibly raped (or worse) by a cadre of angry men whom Stan had been responsible for sending here? It might have sounded like this:

"Hey! Ow. No! He gave me a twenty-five-dollar US savings bond for my thirteenth birthday [which, ironically, probably helped to fund our prisons]! It's almost due to cash out! Uff! We can put it on your commissary account! Oooo!" He'd written on the bond that I was to "use it in good health." I could think of no better way/time.

Backing down the hallway, I loudly proclaimed, "I'm not interested in seeing you guys!" Then I made haste back to my yard. I was sweaty and out of breath when I got back. I thought for sure everyone was watching me reenter the yard, this time with evil intent. You know how paranoid you get sometimes when you're high? Well, imagine that paranoia times one thousand pairs of murderous eyes watching you. Even if it's not real, it's real scary.

Fuck! How could those guys (especially Stan) be so careless? Fuck. Fuck. Fuck. It was hard enough for me to safely assimilate while being as innocuous as possible, just to survive. Now I was expecting a shiv (the pen or pencil from that set would've made a great weapon) to enter my kidney at any moment. I shivered at what else might enter me from behind.

I didn't see Bob. In fact, I never saw him again.

We were summoned to assemble for dinner. I kept a wide berth, walking as close to the guards as possible. Shouldn't I have been doing that anyway? My eyes were darting in every direction. I was just like every other paranoid prisoner in there. Maybe I had taken things too lightly before. Maybe this was how I should have always been . . . on high alert . . . at all times. I was near the bottom rung on the ladder of prey out in this jungle. I was so vulnerable. I was so stupid.

I managed to live through dinner that night, as well as the silverware count—thankfully, all potential weapons (at least newly crafted ones) had been accounted for. I practically sat in one guard's lap during the after-dinner board games and static-filled maximum-volume dueling radio contests. Afterward, I carefully made my way back to my solitary cell. There I felt (and hoped) I was safe. Who knew what word may have been spread around the prison grapevine? It was rapid and decisive, its sentences much more punitive than Judge Stanley Golde had ever doled out.

It wasn't like I could actually talk to anyone about my predicament. I couldn't really see myself beginning a conversation with, "Hey, did you hear any scuttlebutt about my almost-visit with the judge who sentenced you to twenty-five years? Yeah . . . he's been sitting with my family for twenty-five years during Yom Kippur services at Temple Beth Abraham." I did not think that would play.

The next week, I stood with my back to the wall at all times. It was amazing how casually I had previously discounted all the dangers looming around me at any time. I kept my eyes peeled for any unusual gatherings or wayward looks in my direction, though I was woefully unprepared to discern if anything was amiss. I hadn't showered in over two months now, and my raggedy beard was quite full by this time. Not that I was Paul Newman to begin with, but I made myself as unappealing as I could, although I had a lot of competition in that area. Now I was even more afraid of the showers. I could get fucked *and* killed. Or killed and fucked. I didn't know the order I preferred.

I guess things finally settled down a bit, though my thoughts didn't. But really, who knew when a shot-caller was gonna call a strike and snuff the life out of me? The mind did have time to wander a tad in there. God, I wanted out of there so badly. I'd get to the cellblock desk and receive the mournful shrug from my spurned love. Maybe the time had come and he was penalizing me. *Oh please, let this torture end. Peacefully, though.* I skulked around. I always wore a frown. *Shit, maybe if I got shanked, it could speed up the process of getting out of here.*

I began to wonder what it was like to get stabbed. Probably not great. While my high-school classmates were busy pondering their choices ahead—entering law school or maybe taking well-deserved vacations (perhaps a year abroad) upon completing their undergrad studies—I was calculating the advantages of being sliced open by a homemade knife in state prison. Lovely how far I had come.

Chapter 40: Comfortably Numb

The days crept on. You've probably surmised that I survived. One night, after a particularly stress-filled day, I found myself lying on my back, face up like in a coffin. My mattress was on a cement platform five feet up from the floor. I wedged myself into this space and onto my mattress, which left two feet between me and the ceiling. I was in a sort of crypt. I closed my eyes and clasped my hands together at my stomach. I must've looked like a corpse in a morgue.

I could hear the muted wailing sounds of the various caged animals around me. It was a full moon. Things were particularly creepy. I could even hear the coyotes howling in the far-distant hills. The slot I was wedged into began feeling claustrophobic. I could barely turn over. I became more and more focused on this extremely tight space. There was no getting up and strolling into the kitchen for a snack, or into the living room to turn on the TV. No walking outside to look at the moon, or getting into the car and going for a drive. No petting my dog or cuddling with my significant other. Just me in my locked four-foot-by-seven-foot cell. A twenty-eight-square-foot home.

I was getting more and more anxious and began to hyperventilate. There was no red emergency button to push, nor was there a telephone to dial 911. I tried calming myself down by focusing on all the great things I had in my life. The future was going to be bright. This would be just a temporary setback. I would overcome it and thrive. It was how you got up after being knocked down. You know, all the motivational mantras.

There were a couple of nights a week that prisoners got to be DJs as we were locked back in our cells. The music was piped into each cell, and you connected via a thin transistor wire earplug, just like the ones I used to listen to ballgames in Temple just a few years earlier. This night was one of those nights. I didn't generally listen in; I preferred to try to sleep as much as possible to make the time pass quicker. I love music, but I wasn't into it just then. I found it hard to enjoy anything.

For whatever reason, though, tonight I put in the earphones and hoped to be soothed. I found myself enjoying some tasty rock. I love many forms of music, but I felt reached by these sounds. I was calming down and being moved by the music. I think it was the Doobie Brothers' beautiful "South City Midnight Lady." I nodded my head and grooved to the tunes.

Suddenly the entire mood changed. The signal was hijacked, like screeching noise caused by the needle of the record player being dragged over an entire album side, then followed by a bunch of gibberish. I guess it was time to change DJs. Instead of a friendly and mellow handoff, this was more like a hostile pirate takeover—a lot of verbal ranting and raving, yelling, and angry words. Sounds of hate.

The next song I heard was by Sly and the Family Stone. I loved soul music! I began digging on that. But within seconds, the needle again scratched abruptly over the entire album, and what sounded like Aryan Nation preaching filled my earplugs.

The message was violent and full of despair. Sound, whether music or words, is so powerful. Minutes before, I had been calm and reflective, almost nurtured to comfort and rest. Now I became agitated and angry and frustrated. The awful words of hate continued, and I flung the earpiece away in disgust. I felt like weeping. I know it seems trite, but I was on edge . . . on the verge of losing it. The walls were seemingly pressing upon me, like the trash compactor in *Star Wars*.

Lying there, I looked out the heavily barred window overlooking the prison. I could see cellblocks illuminated by the full moon, stretching nearly a mile. These were lined with cells just like mine, prisoners filled with pain and anguish just like me. I could only imagine this vast area of darkness. I had to imagine their pain to be much worse than mine. But I'd had enough. I wanted out. Now!

I began to breathe heavily again. I was panting. Lying down on my back again, I stared straight up into that solid gray slab of cement looming above me. I was really feeling a good sorry for myself. Yes, I was. And I felt so freaking powerless.

Then I began to feel very light headed. I also felt as if my entire body was becoming weightless. I was floating upward into the cement ceiling. I couldn't move my arms and legs. I felt like I was tied up like Gulliver by the Lilliputians. I really had no idea what was going on—all I knew was that I could feel myself rising and being pressed up against the ceiling. Not physically, but my inner soul. I felt that, if I allowed myself, I could shoot up through the ceiling and out into the night.

I envisioned myself looking down at the prison complex from a thousand yards in the sky, like Peter Pan flying above the London lights. Was I dreaming? I didn't think so. A panic attack? Possibly. But it was kind of exciting and also petrifying at the same time. I was like a rocket ready to take off. Just the last tether, and I would be gone. Somehow, in the recesses of my mind (I don't know where), I grasped that this might not have been a great time for this experience. I wanted to physically escape, but that also wasn't a great idea.

I had heard about astral projection. I had heard that if you left your body during astral projection, it was the most vulnerable time. Another spirit could enter and occupy your body while your own spirit was away; this could cause you to have multiple personalities when yours re-entered. Okay. Well, that was a concern. I did not want to share my body with any of the souls that might be hanging around this place. Some were probably just waiting for a fool like me to take off in a flight of fancy; upon my return, I'd have a houseguest in my head. I had seen some wacked-out guys having intense solo conversations with themselves during my stay. Maybe this was why.

I didn't want anything to mess with my earliest possible straightforward exit out of this place. I didn't want any reports that I was having an argument with a new visitor to my brain. I felt I would be at a disadvantage to convince others (including my father, as tolerant as he had been) that I had teleported to Mecca, returned, and was still fine; it was just that I would now be sharing my body with a mass murderer from the 1950s. He had infiltrated me one night in Vacaville.

As potentially amazing as it would have been, I shut myself down and reversed the process. I've tried since then to recreate this astral projection experience, to no avail. Maybe it's for the better.

I put the earphone back in and did not allow myself to fall asleep. When I got up at first light, I looked into my dull steel mirror and was grateful that it only reflected myself back to me.

Across the cell block, I saw a guy who could only be described as a stark raving lunatic. He was carrying on multiple conversations with himself, which were punctuated by sharp jabs into the empty cell, along with yipping and yapping noises. I had noticed him carrying on spasmodically like this for a few days. I thought he might've been detoxing. Maybe he was suffering from a different journey.

Chapter 41: On the Road Again

Finally! My spurned lover delivered the great message! I was to be leaving Vacaville State Prison. Like, in an hour.

No time for long farewells, which weren't necessary anyway. I hopped, skipped, and jumped to retrieve my belongings, all of which fit into one well-worn paper grocery bag—mostly letters, mostly from my dad. I reversed the intake process that I had done seventy days earlier, and waved goodbye to the prisoner still hoarding that sports page on my way out of there. I wonder, is he still doing that some forty years later? It's possible.

I exited the prison into one of those cyclone-fence cages, where my gleaming chariot (in this case, a 1975 Ford LTD) awaited. How beautiful she looked, "Butte County Sheriff" plastered on the side. I was going home. Well, fucked-up Oroville, then home. I had my absolutely glowing reports safely clutched in my fists. I hoped Amber was also on her way back to Butte County. Could this ordeal be over?! The judge had promised to abide by whatever recommendations I had received from Vacaville.

The return trip was far more uneventful than the ride down had been. I was the only prisoner aboard, my own Uber X. They even let me ride without being handcuffed. I had prepared a story in case we spotted any of my parents' friends; I was going to pretend I was writing an article for the college newspaper and was doing a police ride-along. This would've been wholly unnecessary, as the Oakland Jewish yenta gossip tree had already spread a new forest with the manure of my arrest.

"My son the doctor!"

"My son the lawyer!"

"My son the state prisoner. But it's not a felony!" my parents could only reply.

I was escorted back to the area where my imprisonment had all begun. The rooms were the same—full, but with a whole new group of people. In one section, there were a couple of guys my age. I quickly figured out that they had also just returned from Vacaville. They had served the same "evaluation" sentence as I had and were a day or two ahead of me in the process. They explained that now they were just waiting to see the judge again for their formal sentencing. It was nice to have some guys in there who could actually answer a few questions. It was like when Bob had helped me out so much the first time I had been in this place.

I hung out with these guys. They were all friends from Los Angeles, also students at Chico State, and had also sold drugs to the same undercover narc, although they had sold far larger quantities—it would've been hard to have sold less than I had. I liked them. We might have been friends under other circumstances. Here, it was still mostly just survival. Of course, we showed each other our reports from Vacaville. Mine was by far the most positive and promising of a release. I was the head of my class!

Our range of activities was limited; we played cards sometimes as we waited for our court dates. One of the guys shared that at least we were lucky to have survived Vacaville. He added, "Unlike the guy from Butte County we saw murdered last week."

They went on to describe a horrific stabbing. The cut began at the victim's throat and continued across his Adam's apple to the other side of his throat up to his ear. They told me he had fallen like a rag doll, that it had all started because of a drug deal that had gone south. They said the guy's name was Bob.

I fell to my cot like a rag doll.

I hadn't yet had a lot of experience dealing with death in my life. It was a feeling I was unused to. It wasn't like I had really spent a lot of time with Bob, and most of that hadn't been great fun. But he had helped me very much during a very difficult episode of my young life. I shared my stories of Bob with these guys and shed a tear. I guess you could argue that Bob's life had always been on a fast track to a bad ending. It was tragic, nonetheless. "If not for the grace of God," I repeated to myself.

I worried and wondered if I would get beaten up by someone for crying about Bob. I didn't care.

The next couple of days were spent slowly waiting for our court dates. My parents figured out that I had been transferred when they went to Vacaville and found that I was no longer there. That must have freaked them out, but they were pleased that things seemed to be moving forward. They told Brooke I was in Oroville. I didn't know where Amber was.

My new friends finally had their court date and were set free by my judge. Boy, that was both fantastic and extremely envy inducing. I had never actually seen anyone leave one of these places. It was encouraging to see it happen, but I wanted to see it happen to me. And to Amber!

I was nearing the end of this grueling marathon. I felt like I was in a horror movie . . . one where you try to run toward something, but the camera makes it feel as if your destination is further and further away.

Little did I know, the monster in this horror movie was about to rear its ugly head. My old friend and parole officer, Gustine, came back into my life.

Cornering me, he asked about my experiences in Vacaville. I could sense him getting excited, trying to dredge up any material he could use against me. He circled me and began asking little questions in his obsequious manner. I tried to remain cool—after all, I had that fantastic report in my back pocket.

Gustine quickly shot his load and became furious. Boy, I must've represented every suppressed thing he had either hated or desired in his life. I've never had such an effect on anyone before or since. He ranted and raved.

My old PO discounted all my positive reports from Vacaville. Then he pulled a real fucked-up maneuver: he asked for a court delay. I was supposed to go before the court the very next day, and Gustine knew the judge was going on vacation for two weeks the day after that. He got his delay, and this left me waiting again. I was stuck—two more weeks of unnecessary and mindless waiting. Fourteen fucking more mind-fucking days. I was in a foul mood, but I had to keep my wits about me.

At this time, there was a new, younger class of convicts in this jail. Teenagers. Teen Ragers. Lots of anger and testosterone filled these waiting cells. The leader was that guy I mentioned who looked like a young Axl Rose. Maybe it was him. This was before Guns N' Roses had hit it big. "Axl" orchestrated daily competitions and near-hourly fist fights. Some of these struggles went on mere inches from my face. Our leader mused how detached I appeared. I just knew that if I expressed any emotions, I'd be dragged into this mess.

I was left out of it. I used my brain instead of my brawn to avoid trouble. What a shitty way to begin the summer.

Chapter 42: Judgment Day

Finally, my day in court. Gustine could not delay any longer, and it turns out he didn't want to—he had planned it so that Amber and I would be seen again in front of the judge back to back.

I got myself all spiffed up (by that I mean I wasn't wearing something that had "property of" stenciled across the front and down my legs) and was brought to the secure holding area just off the courtroom. I was alone. I looked out the small window and into the courtroom.

There she was! Amber! She was alive. She looked okay. From here, she appeared ever so slight, so vulnerable. I wanted to hold her.

Instead, I could only watch through a thick, bulletproof steel-reinforced window measuring three by ten inches. I couldn't hear anything going on inside the courtroom. Amber's sisters were there, and they were crying hysterically. Then I saw Amber break down sobbing. What the fuck?

Just as suddenly, everyone's mood changed. Amber flashed a smile I hadn't seen in the months since we were arrested. Our lawyer seemed to be congratulating her—although I couldn't be sure, as I'd never seen him on the winning side. But . . . now she was being brought toward my area, nodding her head happily. The bailiffs opened the door, and I had a second with her before my turn in front of the judge. I grabbed her and hugged her.

"I'm free!" she squealed.

I was so happy for her. We had only seconds, but we searched each other's eyes and knew there was still so much more to say. What an ordeal. The world seemed like it just might right itself again. I had to go, but it looked like the end was near.

Then I was brought into the courtroom. I stood in front of the judge—the same judge who had just set Amber free, the same judge who had freed the other young guys a couple of weeks earlier. He had just returned from vacation—surely he'd be in a good mood, or at least a fair one.

Things began without much fanfare. Legal procedural mumblings. Papers being shuffled. Things were proceeding in an orderly manner. Our lawyer (mine only, now) began to defend me, recounting my very positive reports from Vacaville. The district attorney once again waived his right to counter. Things were looking good.

My judgment was about to be rendered when my dear friend Gustine stood up. Gustine had orchestrated that Amber and I would be seen consecutively in court, and he had a plan for just that. He had delayed my appearance until Amber could arrive back from her prison stint. Now, he argued that we should "not be allowed to simply stroll off into the morning sun hand in hand . . . together."

Everything came to a grinding halt. The court clerk stopped typing. Shuffling of papers ceased. It was suddenly very quiet.

The judge pondered for a moment. A long moment. Gustine, the frustrated lawyer, had seemed to make a point. The judge, although reluctant, agreed with his request.

We were outplayed. My attorney had gone up to the plate and kept the bat firmly planted on his shoulder . . . dare I say, yet again?

I was sentenced to an additional six months. Glory, fuck me. That stung. It was so hard to see everyone. To be that close to my freedom. To see it. Then, *bam*! They literally slammed the doors on me. Turning around, I saw the disappointment on my parents' faces yet again.

I was led back to the holding area off the courtroom. Amber was gone. I was brought back to the jail. Now that I had an official sentence, I was told to pack up. I'd be moving to a new section of the Butte County Jail. It had to be better than where I'd just been . . . I hoped.

First, though, I got to visit with my parents. They were obviously as disappointed as I was. My dad assured me that he wasn't done fighting. I believed him, but I was very down. Then my lawyer came in. He said that he had just come from the district attorney's office, where the DA had suggested to him that we should file for a modification. This was a legal term for an appeal to the judge to possibly adjust the sentence. The DA said he would not oppose this in court—the guy ostensibly against me was representing me more effectively than my attorney.

"Let's do this immediately!" I said, to which my lawyer replied that it might be viewed more favorably if we waited a few weeks. I implored him to begin the procedures that very day. "What have we got to lose?"

And then, just like that, it was time for us to go. I don't know where everyone else went, but I went to gather up my gear and move to outdoor quarters, where all the other Butte County inmates, a collection of the town drunks, lived. Liquor-store thieves. Old, redneck, simple-minded, lifetime fuck-ups and failures. There was even a cattle rustler in there.

I was shown into a dormitory-style barracks of about sixty or so army-style cots with small open quarters around each one. It was an open floor plan. Prisoners could spend up to a year in this place. I was scheduled to remain here for the rest of 1978. If Arnold Gustine were to have his way, I'd be in here forever.

I was able to walk outside to a fifty-foot-wide patch of scrabbly lawn. It was surrounded by buildings topped, yet again, with barbed wire. The bathrooms were separate from the sleeping area. That was nice—they were not. Still no individual stalls, and they stank of piss and shit. No AC, and it was hot in there—like, steamy, humid, over-one-hundred-degrees, no-insulation hot. You still had to shit while people were shitting right next to you. I continued my no-showering policy, not so much afraid now, just mad and depressed.

I had very few conversations. This may have been (including the guards) the least intelligent group of people I've ever had the horror of spending any amount of time around. Were these really my peers?

But then again, who was I to judge? I got to sit there and think about the celebration for Amber's release going on a few miles away. I could visualize it. I ached to be part of it, which made this all the more excruciating.

I thought of the days around this time last summer when we had all gone to the Sacramento River, gently floating down it (with our dogs in tow, of course) for glorious hours at a time. Those beginning days of our relationship had been great. These were not. Plus, I could not possibly think of Amber doing this with other guys. I wrote long letters to her professing my undying love. I felt like that unwashed Unabomber letter-writer guy I had helped in Vacaville.

Chapter 43: "Car Wash"

I got word in the morning that I had been chosen for the coveted job: washing the always very dusty Butte County Sheriff vehicles. The "chosen people" indeed! This caused mild consternation among the sharpest minds back at the dorm. Apparently drug dealers were not up for consideration for these positions; also apparently, these decision-makers hadn't dealt with the persuasive powers of my father.

So here I was, out in the sun every day washing cars. The temperature always hovered around a hundred degrees, or so it seemed. Asphalt and metal only reflect heat. The water from the hose was refreshing—although not as much as the Sacramento River. I spent time thinking of Amber, imagining dozens of guys ogling her in her bikini as she floated down that river. And who knew what else could happen? These thoughts were like torture for me. A different type of water torture.

I tried to focus on my fleet. I had four police cruisers to keep clean for new arrestees, and I took pride in my task. I was actually outside the entire jail, no fences surrounding me. I was in the jail parking lot, where no one monitored me for hours at a time. Between washing the cars (supercharged 1977 Dodge Challengers), I sat under a ten-foot-high bush and read or napped. One day my lawyer came by, looked at me, and told me my life "didn't look too bad." What a dipshit. (I felt bad for all his other clients.) I implored him to begin the sentence modification process for me to be seen again in front of the judge.

True, I was getting a great tan. I was mostly stripped down to my boxer shorts and was working hard scrubbing the cars. I had zero body fat. I still had long hair and a healthy beard. Rather fetching, I must say. Quite a catch. Now if only I weren't a convicted felon—I mean, convicted of a misdemeanor—I'd be someone to bring home to Papa. It would be difficult to meet parents, or court anyone properly. Anyway, the only relationship I was interested in was the one I felt had been prematurely interrupted by this silly jail thing. I preferred to end things (if end they must) on my/our own terms and in our own time. Let the relationship live or die of its own volition.

Chapter 44: You're Still a Young Man

June 23, 1978. My Birthday.

It's my party, and I'll cry if I want to. Cry if I want to, cry if I want to. You would cry too if it happened to you.

It was my twenty-third birthday. I always thought that turning twenty-three on the twenty-third would be kind of special. I was not wrong.

I was celebrating in a rather small, private room. My parents were there, as was Leanne, my former girlfriend from junior high and then through high school and the first year of college (remember her?). That seemed like a lifetime ago now. Leanne's parents' home had been a sanctuary for me during our high school years. I'd spent a lot of time there, and I was always welcomed graciously by her father, though her mom was a bit wary of me, even before my first little drug-related run-in with the law. We were not a romantic couple anymore, but we had stayed the best of friends. Leanne had made me my favorite apple pie. Oh yes, she could cook—though to my regret, there were no little escape saws hidden inside the pie.

Leanne was literally the girl next door—well, the girl from down the street. An American classic, 1970s version. Blonde, big blue eyes, long straight hair parted down the middle. Great figure. Freckles and a ready smile. But she wasn't smiling much right now. The event was rather muted, the conversation a bit stilted. The most we could manage was reminiscing about the surprise party she had thrown for me at her parents' house five years earlier, on my eighteenth birthday. I remember us dancing to the brand new Tower of Power album, featuring the song "What Is Hip?" along with dozens of our friends and making out throughout the night.

At today's party, the elephant in the room was the half-dozen other guests surrounding us. These were my jailers. My parents and Leanne did their best to keep things upbeat, but we weren't able to entirely relax around these people. They were not particularly mean, but nonetheless, it was uncomfortable. It wasn't my very best summer thus far.

I did get to visit with Leanne alone for a bit. We talked about our lives and current love situations. She had just graduated from San Diego State University and was looking to extend her education with a master's degree somewhere in the Bay Area; I had just been allowed to extend my prison term in the Butte County Jail. She was trying to figure out the future with her long-term boyfriend after she graduated; I was trying to hear back from my girlfriend in a letter. There was no hanky-panky between us, although I'm sure my parents would've loved for us to get back together. She was a very good catch.

After a couple of hours, they had to leave. I was left with a big hole in my soul for the rest of the day. Leanne told me later that they all had driven the two hours home—including a stop at the Nut Tree for lunch—without anyone uttering a single word. That was a good friend and person. Still is.

Chapter 45: Mystery Train

The long and brutally hot days ever so slowly crept on by. It was two days until Independence Day. That had taken on an entirely new meaning for me.

There I was sitting under my tree, reading my two-hundredth or so book. One of the cops had "tipped" me thirty-five cents by buying me a Coke out of the vending machines. It was a nice gesture. I took a sip and tilted my head up. Focusing my eyes far across the valley, I saw a long, slow train going to who knows where. Who cared? I gave it many destinations.

Boy, I would have loved to cross that expanse of meadow and make the mile or so trek to hop that train. I could have. I could have been gone for several hours before anyone really caught wind of it. They still wouldn't actually know which direction I'd gone. It was so tempting. I mean, wouldn't it be amazing to show up wherever Amber might be? To glide down that river, or more.

Luckily, the un-sunburnt portion of my muddled mind seized control of itself. This would *not* have been a good idea. Whatsoever. But with so much time on my hands, it became increasingly difficult to suppress these thoughts and accompanying desires.

Chapter 46: Born In the U.S.A.

July 4, 1978.

The actual Independence Day, and I was still in prison. Nothing independent about today for me. No fireworks. No barbecues. No beaches or mountains or rivers to glide down. No baseball. No bikinis. No much of anything. No real difference from any other non–Independence Day in here.

I take that back. I was recruited by the two other guys who had also been allowed outside the jail. They were the gardeners. They corralled me to help them in picking boysenberries. They had big plans to use these berries and their connections in the kitchen to have a pie made without proper authorization. I was promised my fair share of this pie, the creation of which was going to require multiple contributors to pull off. I really didn't care, but what else did I have going on? It wasn't like I was busy party-hopping in the Hamptons with P. Diddy. (Maybe P. Diddy is gonna wish he could trade places with me the next July 4.)

It was going to be a busy day for the patrol officers, so my squadron was out patrolling the streets. I made my way across the lot to the bramble bush. It was a particularly prickly shrub, and the heat was stifling; I only stayed and picked berries so I wouldn't be singled out as a killjoy (and not actually be killed). Also, I wasn't supposed to be away from my car-washing area, I guess in case there were any emergency calls for clean cop cars. That part of disobeying the authorities appealed to me.

I picked my allotment of berries and placed them into the small valise provided to me for smuggling back into our compound. No one seemed to give one shit what we might be carrying back into the jail.

We could've been hiding a cache of AK-47s for all they knew, or, like Bob (may he rest in peace), a buttful of ragweed.

Many hours later, on what turned out to be the least independent of all my Independence Days, I was back on my cot. I guess the inmates in the kitchen had pulled off their participation in Pie-gate, because I was sensing a buzz rolling through the dorm. Along with the buzz, I saw a piece of pie heading down the cots, hand by hand. Frankly, I had forgotten about it. Many of the guys must have been dying to take a bite, but they honorably passed it all the way down the line to me.

I took inventory of my piece. It was quite generous. Slowly, I took a bite. When I looked up, I was surrounded by some very expectant faces.

I shared with the rest of the guys. The only thing good about that pie was that it was illicit. It actually tasted quite horrible; the kind thought was there, but it was lacking so many of the ingredients which would truly make it taste homemade. Watching the others covet their portions ever so gratefully, it got me to thinking of how many Fourth of Julys (and how many other holidays) these souls had spent in places like this—and how many more they would in the future.

I had taken my freedom for granted. I could only imagine what others were up to today. Again, we had no phones, no TV, no fireworks! No excited plans to get together with friends and family and eat barbecue until we were stuffed. No extra care for my dog. I hoped he would be comforted through the loud noises. Amber was out, so he would be with her—although I couldn't really be sure of that. I didn't know where she would be.

It was easy to share with my other freedomless soul brothers. I really shared their pain today.

Chapter 47: Tell You Something

It was my Nana's birthday. She was my favorite person in the world. I'm certain her feelings for me were mutual. Unabashed love existed between her and my family. She and I had a connection that I've rarely experienced again in my life. She never judged me, and always championed any cause I sought to undertake.

Nana worked so hard all her life. She met my grandfather when she was a ticket-taker at a Brooklyn movie theater box office in 1917, when she was fourteen. He was kind of a bum, a bum she would end up supporting her entire life. She was a brilliant mother, fair and honest and loving and strong. I wish she had been my mother; unlike my actual mother, she stood up for me when my brother was bullying me. She was the only person with whom I felt truly protected.

Nana lived in Los Angeles, and spent most (if not all) of her extra money coming up to Oakland to visit us. A ticket between Los Angeles and Oakland on PSA Airlines cost seven dollars; I think she earned $1.65 an hour. When Nana visited, my mom would let her take over—thank God. Nana would whip out the waffle iron. Until much later in my life, I thought making waffles was reserved for fancy chefs from four-star restaurants. She made potato pancakes and other delights. My mom could cook, but she never did it with a smile on her face. Nana always greeted my dad with warmth and respect. They enjoyed sitting together at the end of my dad's day and having a drink before dinner. He adored her.

To not be able to see Nana or even call her was unthinkable. I knew she had to be aware of my recent absence, but we couldn't tell her why.

She wouldn't have slept a wink if she had known where I really was. I could not wait to see her.

Chapter 48: Loan Me a Dime

July 8, 1978.

It was Leanne's birthday. Probably no coincidence that the two best girls I knew up to this point were born a day apart on the calendar. We had always celebrated Leanne's birthday around Nana's birthday celebration. Those two loved each other—Nana loved anyone who loved me, and everyone loved Nana.

Nana would not have loved some of these hick guards. One was a small, skinny, older guy with a receding hairline, gold wire-rimmed glasses, and a bushy mustache to counter his very weak chin. I would later learn he was in cahoots with Gustine to dig up dirt on me. When he told me what a particular loser I was, I politely pointed out that I would be in here for a few months of my life, whereas his working here eight to ten hours a day for the next thirty-five years would add up to roughly being in jail for twelve years.

I did not get a gold star for my math prowess that day. More like a purple bruise.

I wish I could have visited Leanne on her birthday, like she ever-so-kindly had for mine two weeks earlier. There wasn't much to report on the Amber frontier either. I would have loved a letter or ten each day, but I don't really remember a letter at all. If things were reversed, I would have written her every day. As it was, I still did. Once again, these letters had to be disguised as correspondences to other people. Part of Amber's release orders (and soon to be part of mine) was that we were not to have any contact with each other for the next five years! She was complying a tad too stringently for my taste. It made me extremely distraught, and I was quite depressed.

Chapter 49: Don't Stop Believin'

I was sitting under the Burning Bush—this was what I called the shrub near the parking lot where I washed patrol cars, because even under its touch of shade, it was 105 degrees outside—when my attorney pulled into the lot. I couldn't help to notice that he was driving a brand new convertible BMW. He was passing by and saw me sitting there reading.

"Hey!" he said, not for the first time. "Looks like a pretty good setup you got going on here for yourself. I might trade you," he added with a chuckle. He *should* have been here, I thought—for malpractice. Impersonating a lawyer.

"Yeah. Not really in the mood for jokes, I guess," I mumbled back from underneath my shrub. "What I am in the mood for is getting the fuck out of here. Let's do the modification!" *I mean, why the fuck do I have to be the one to continue pushing him to do this?*

He tried to counter that it was probably too early to file, but I insisted that I didn't care—it was the time. I wanted to do it *now*. What the fuck did I have to lose?

Finally, he agreed to petition the court for a hearing date. Unbeknownst to me, my father was furiously working the phones behind the scenes with Gustine. In yet another one of his lies, the latter agreed to remain neutral and allow the judge and DA to decide my fate.

As my attorney left me under the scrub bush, he told me, "Oh yeah. This will cost another fifteen hundred."

I had never seen a guy say or do less and charge more in my young life until I worked in Hollywood.

Chapter 50: Dear Mr. Fantasy

July 14, 1978. A few days later.

Lo and behold, we got our court date. It occurred rather quickly, all things falling into place—it was set for July 18, a mere four days from then. The waiting time was now all the more excruciating.

My old guard buddy grew increasingly present. He was sniffing about, trying to dredge up any dirt on me, his gills gasping for air like a fish tossed on a hot rock. He attempted to unsettle me and jigger my cage as much as he could, trying to get me to act out toward him. He'd pull up into the police car parking lot, throw me his keys, and say, "If you've got some extra time, maybe you could wash my car." Then he'd laugh and say lovely things like, "Looks like we'll get to spend Christmas with a kike this year." Oh yeah. He was a gem.

Allegedly, Gustine was complying with his agreement with my father, wherein he'd stand by and let the judge decide my future. After all, that was the way I was originally promised to be sentenced, according to the reports from Vacaville. But Gustine had stuck his pudgy fingers into the dyke on that one, and he had no intention of withdrawing them now. Even at this late hour, this hound was still trying to dig up a bone.

The next four days, I tried to sleep as much as possible to once again make the time pass quickly. In fact, I was so wound up, I found it extremely difficult to eat, read, or even shit. Freedom was an actual, maybe even impending, possibility . . . again. It was so daunting, so tantalizingly near. All I could do was sit in the dark void and wait. And wait.

I had just under a hundred hours to kill. Each minute was like an hour. Outside, there was only one small patch of lawn at this place, so I worked on my tan. That's about all I could do. I pretended I was on the beach in Malibu. There was little else to distract the churning thoughts torturing my mind.

I could actually be released as soon as July 18! Or . . . not until next year. If it was to be July, I would actually be able to register for school in September and make a step toward a more productive life. If not, I'd miss another semester, not to mention Thanksgiving and the other family holidays, like "the kike holiday Hanukkah," as my friendly guard often reminded me—even as he mispronounced it as "Hankunah."

This could set me back a full year. This was a huge issue. When you've only lived twenty-three years, one of them constitutes nearly 5 percent of your life. Fuck all that. I just wanted to walk. It had been all I had thought about for months . . . the fantasy of moving on out of all this bullshit.

Chapter 51: With or Without You

July 18, 1978. Four days later.

They handed me back the pants and shirt I had worn some five months earlier, the same ones I had relinquished to the jail's property room. They barely hung onto my frame. I had lost nearly thirty pounds. My Famolare shoes still fit, though. The heavy, wavy, thick rubber soles had not even separated from the upper leather part as so many did. Maybe this could be a future advertising campaign for Famolare shoes.

It was 9:00 a.m. My day in court! Again. I entered the same area where I had last seen Amber. Peering into the courtroom, I saw that it was empty save for my ever-loyal, supportive, and faithful father. He smiled broadly and gave me a full Fonzie double thumbs-up.

Then I was led in and seated at the defendant's table in front, where my attorney joined me. Across the aisle was the district attorney. He was a fair-enough-seeming guy. Medium height, build, and age. I turned around frequently to smile at my dad; about the fourth time I turned to look at him, I saw Gustine enter.

Oh shit. I didn't think there was any need for him to be there. Hadn't he had enough? His thick folder that didn't hide his thick belly, but he was trying. He must've gorged himself even extra on the previous Fourth-of-July barbecues—not to mention every other day after that. Waddling on, he huffed down to a seat in the front row of the gallery.

Again, there was a lot of noise: paper shuffling, the clickety-clack sounds from an actual typewriter, and bits of muted conversing. Several coughs sounded; the wooden chairs we were sitting in and the wood benches in the back squeaked. Finally, the judge entered. We all stood up respectfully. He was handed the docket and murmured his assent to begin the proceedings.

My lawyer started and made his case for my release—I think. It was so tentative that his viewpoint was hard to pinpoint. I still believe he used my case as a hedge to gain favors for his firm or for another case that his firm was arguing. His position was acknowledged by the judge, and we moved forward.

The DA presented the people's side. He seemed very interested in allowing me to be released! I'll never forget his exact words: "It is the Dog Days of summer, and I believe that enough time has been served and punishment meted out," he told the judge. He added that he felt I had a strong support system in place and that little more could be accomplished by my spending more time in jail. In fact, he felt "it could do more harm to the defendant's character if he continues to remain in custody." I agreed wholeheartedly. I loved him. I wished he was my lawyer.

The judge listened, then asked them if that was all they wanted to say. He grabbed his gavel and was about to pronounce his decision when I heard a bench groan behind me, its 250-pound occupant lifting his five-foot-five-inch frame off it.

Among many of the frustrations Mr. Gustine possessed, one was clearly his thwarted ambition to be a lawyer. He cleared his throat and, in his best Perry Mason imitation, asked if he could approach the bench. The judge seemed perplexed, yet he granted him access. Gustine waddled forward, opened his folder, and stroked his devilish goatee. Then he launched into a forty-five-minute diatribe describing why I should not be released—in fact, why I would be a menace to society if I were *ever* released.

It was like an infomercial about the dangers of a free-roaming Richard Beren. Heck, *I* wanted me locked up during his oral dissertation. I sounded like a total asshole. Among the many incidents he droned on about was the "time [I] had answered a guard with a mathematical retort." He repeated what I had stated to the old guard, that "I would be out of here in mere months, whereas if he spent his [I'm certain I said 'miserable' here] thirty-year career here, then ten of his years [I'm pretty sure I said twelve] would actually be inside jail." I was also accused of telling another guard that I was to receive a $400,000 inheritance upon my twenty-fifth birthday (if so, I'm still waiting—my sixty-fifth birthday is next year). Okay, so I could be found guilty of being a fairly obnoxious asshole. But I was pretty sure I was no danger to society . . . unless being a dickhead is a crime.

Gustine droned on and on, to the point that I tuned out his words and could only see his Adam's apple bobbing up and down. Thankfully, the judge seized his moment when my PO paused to swipe some sweat off his perspiring forehead and jowls. "With all due respect, Mr. Gustine, are you finished?"

Hearing an affirmative answer from this F. Lee Bailey wannabe, the judge thanked him. Then he turned to me and asked me what my future plans would be if I were to be released today.

I had *not* expected to have to speak. Gulping hard, I felt my own Adam's apple negotiate with my exceedingly shrivelled throat; then I said that I would head directly to Oakland and immediately start working for my father. "I need to pay him back," I told the judge. I added that I would be living with my parents in their home; that I promised to abide by all the laws of the land and the restrictions placed upon me, to be a good and productive citizen for as long as I should live. Most of this was true. (I still owe my father for the legal fees.)

The judge nodded and seemed to approve of my answer. Mostly, I think he approved of its brevity. "It is time for water to find its own level," he said, "and it's also time to set you free." The gavel banged down loud. "Time served."

John Bonham never sounded so good.

I was free to go, effective immediately! Like *right then*, motherfuckers!

I was stunned, but I quickly recovered. I thanked the judge, and the DA, and my lawyer (even though he had done very little). By now my dad had raced to my side, and we gave each other a huge bear hug just inches from Gustine's supremely pissed-off person. My dad was practically in tears, but I couldn't see them through my own. I felt better for my dad than I did for myself—and I was feeling pretty damn great.

You see other guys get out of there, and you know it's going to happen for you, but until it actually does, it doesn't mean anything. This feeling was delicious, made even more so because it was happening in front of Gustine. He was furious. I thought he was going to choke on his little red bow tie. At least, I think it was red—his face sure was, but the tie was mostly hidden behind several of his quivering chins.

I still had to go back and get formally processed out of this mother-fucker, but I was officially on my way out! July 18 was my turn. It was such an amazing feeling to be the one right now. When I was imprisoned, it had felt like I was carrying those steel bars and cement walls on my back everywhere I walked. Now they were about to be lifted.

My father and I reluctantly released each other from our arms, and I went back inside to be formally processed into my freedom. It was not like on TV, where people just stride out the front door. That would've have suited me fine—there was absolutely nothing I had to retrieve, and I didn't need to bid adieu to my dormitory. Plus, going back could be dangerous—dudes often got pissed when someone other than themselves got out, and this was the last time they could address any pending vendettas. I had no such enemies (that I knew of), but I did understand the envy of witnessing someone walk out the doors and never return.

The jailers knew to take extra precautions when they escorted me back to my area in the dorm, then away again. I got a few half-hearted well wishes, and more than one "See you in a few weeks!" That caused me to shiver and shake my head "Noooooooooo." They weren't kidding.

They'd seen it happen more than a few times. One guy offered me his *Dianetics* book—thinking it was about weight loss, I demurred.

Twenty minutes later (twenty *long* minutes, when you are technically free but still physically behind bars), I found myself at the final exit door to freedom. Alas, whose face did I see first, once on the other side of that door? Oh yes. It was my friendly, fat-faced probation officer, tie mercifully unleashed: Mr. A.(hole) Gustine.

"In my office. *Now!*" These were the first words I heard exiting the jail after five months of imprisonment.

I looked over at my father, who stood next to this abomination of a man. Two such diverse human beings. My dad and I gave each other a look of support and strength; then, I trudged reluctantly into Gustine's office. I had sat in this very office before, where he had compiled every possible thing he could dredge up to assassinate my character. I had trusted him once. This time, I knew better.

He began slyly, gently inquiring about my immediate plans. I took a deep breath and repeated verbatim what I had just expressed to the judge. "I'm moving to Oakland. I'm going to live with my parents and work for my father."

Gustine grunted, "And then what?"

I calmly answered, "I plan on enrolling in a Bay Area college to complete my interrupted education."

Then he slipped in a curveball: "Will you be seeing Ms. Jenson any time soon?"

"Oh, no sir," I lied—or at least I hoped it was a lie. Still, I did not have any actual plans to see her, so technically I was okay.

Gustine stammered, stuttered, and turned beet red. Then he swallowed (I witnessed each of the half-dozen chins move up and down) and politely offered to continue to be my probation officer, if I would like.

I almost did a spit take. I certainly would have, had I previously been offered some water. Fortunately, though, the judge had kindly allowed our petition to change the county where my probation would be overseen. We had requested the friendly confines of Alameda County—home court advantage. The real advantage was having my dad's best friend, Judge Golde, put one of his finest disciples in charge. My five-year probation would consist of exactly one visit to see this guy, and that would be that. Ah! It was good to be back to my entitled ways. I was still under probation, but the only way I would be affected was if I broke the law. Or should I say, if I were *caught* breaking the law.

Gustine fumed. But I had learned to be smart (occasionally) and repeated *exactly* the words I had said in court a few minutes earlier. If I hadn't, he would have thrown me back in jail (for up to five years!) for contempt of court, then claimed I had lied under oath. (Which, of course, I had. Kind of a sneaky fuck.)

I excused myself from his clutches. My dad almost bowled me over on his way past me into Gustine's office. He closed the door behind him. I sat outside, but I vividly imagined the ass-reaming he had been waiting months to deliver. It basically could have been titled "*He* May Be on Probation, but *I'm* Not." The theme was "Stay the fuck away."

Afterward, my dad and I pushed open the heavy double doors and strode out into the sunshine of the beautiful July morning. The freedom of movement was astonishing. I could walk at any pace right to my father's sparkling clean Cadillac. The last time I rode in this car had been a somber affair. This time I got into the plush leather front seat and said, "Let's get the fuck out of here."

Away we drove. We had no cell phones, so we weren't able to tell anyone the news yet, but who cared? We were free! I say "we" because my dad was with me all the time. Inside and out.

"What do you want to do?" he asked me.

Hell, I had not been asked what I wanted to do as anything but a pure hypothetical in months. I immediately got a 50 percent on this test. "I want to go get my dog and hopefully see Amber," I answered.

Those were the answers he'd expected but did not want to hear. Of course I needed to get Walker, but Amber was most certainly not the best choice at that moment. He reluctantly drove me to Brooke's boyfriend's house to retrieve my dog. He didn't think I would really see Amber. I mean, just how stupid (and horny) was I?

There were a few people gathered there when we arrived. I don't remember why. Maybe I had called from a pay phone along the way to have someone (again, hopefully Amber) bring Walker to me. And sure enough, my cherished dog arrived! He greeted me like a long-lost friend. The feeling of rubbing his ears and hugging him was ecstasy; he rolled on his back, and I scratched his belly as he moaned and whimpered.

Amber had brought him to me. She, unlike Walker, was more standoffish. I guess she wasn't ready to have her belly rubbed or her ears scratched (although I tried).

We sat around awkwardly outside for a few minutes. Someone suggested that all of us (sans my dad, who was nervously waiting in his car) get in the hot tub. I was more than game. Less than an hour out of jail and I was gonna see girls in bikinis? Yes. I could do that! I liked freedom. I wanted even more (as in fewer clothes, or better yet none), but Amber was freaked out. After a few minutes, my dad came outside and said we should really get going. I reluctantly agreed.

We grabbed Walker and headed off to get my car. My dad, smarter than I, was relieved; so was Walker, who was also smarter. I must admit, it was a good feeling to head out of town without any further trouble. I felt the weight lifting from my shoulders more and more with each passing mile out of Chico.

We arrived at a small independent mechanic's shop my father had found months previously. Here he'd had them restore my then three-year-old 1974 baby-blue convertible Karmann Ghia to pristine shape. We went out to the back, and the old guy proudly whipped back the cloth tarp. There she was, sitting face out and smiling all pretty-like at me. It seemed like a story where you might find an untouched classic bathtub Porsche in the back of a Kentucky farmhouse. My Ghia purred to life. She was ready to go. I would keep that car for another thirty-five years, until I lost it in a suspicious fire. Gustine?

I loaded Walker in and followed my dad down the highway out of Butte County. Good fucking riddance. We made plans to rendezvous and grab a bite at the Nut Tree. I followed my dad off the highway and found myself about one mile from the Vacaville State Prison. Months earlier, I had been across the highway sitting in that institution, shackled and certain that a dramatic prison escape was about to occur. Weird.

We pulled into the friendly and familiar oak tree old-time parking lot, the gravel crunching under my new tires. I let Walker out for a stroll; he seemed as happy as I was. Such simple pleasures. Afterward, I left him in my car (under the shade of a big oak tree and with a full bowl of water) and went in to grab lunch . . . whatever I wanted. Walker whimpered and whined. He was not happy—the last time I had left him had been for months.

It was during lunch that my dad began to tell me why neither my mom nor anyone else from our family had come with him to pick me up. My Nana (the most beloved person in my life) had suffered a massive heart attack days earlier. My mom and brother had immediately flown to her bedside in the hospital in Los Angeles.

This news crushed me. It hit me harder than anything I had suffered the past few months. I had not told Nana about my predicament. She would never have stopped worrying for a second. I would have feared causing her a stroke.

My dad asked me if/when I wanted to go to L.A., and I replied, "Immediately."

It would take ten books to describe the pure love and adoration I felt for Nana. She worked her fingers to the bone. She never complained. She was fair and strong. I rarely saw her getting mad at me. Why would she? I'd never do anything to upset her. And if I did, I would apologize, and be forgiven, in an instant.

As we finished lunch, I was in a daze. We made our way back to our cars. Walker was fine—he got a lot of leftovers, as I had lost my appetite. A few hours later, I was on a plane to visit my Nana. It had been quite a day.

I joined my family around Nana's bedside at the hospital. She was a fighter. I got that sweet smile. I know she loved me the most, and I knew I loved her the most. She knew something had been going on with me, but would never have said anything to make the situation more uncomfortable. My family was grateful to see me, but very mournful in the hospital room.

I stayed with my mom in Los Angeles for the next two weeks. Nana was recovering. Now, it was time for me to recover for some lost time.

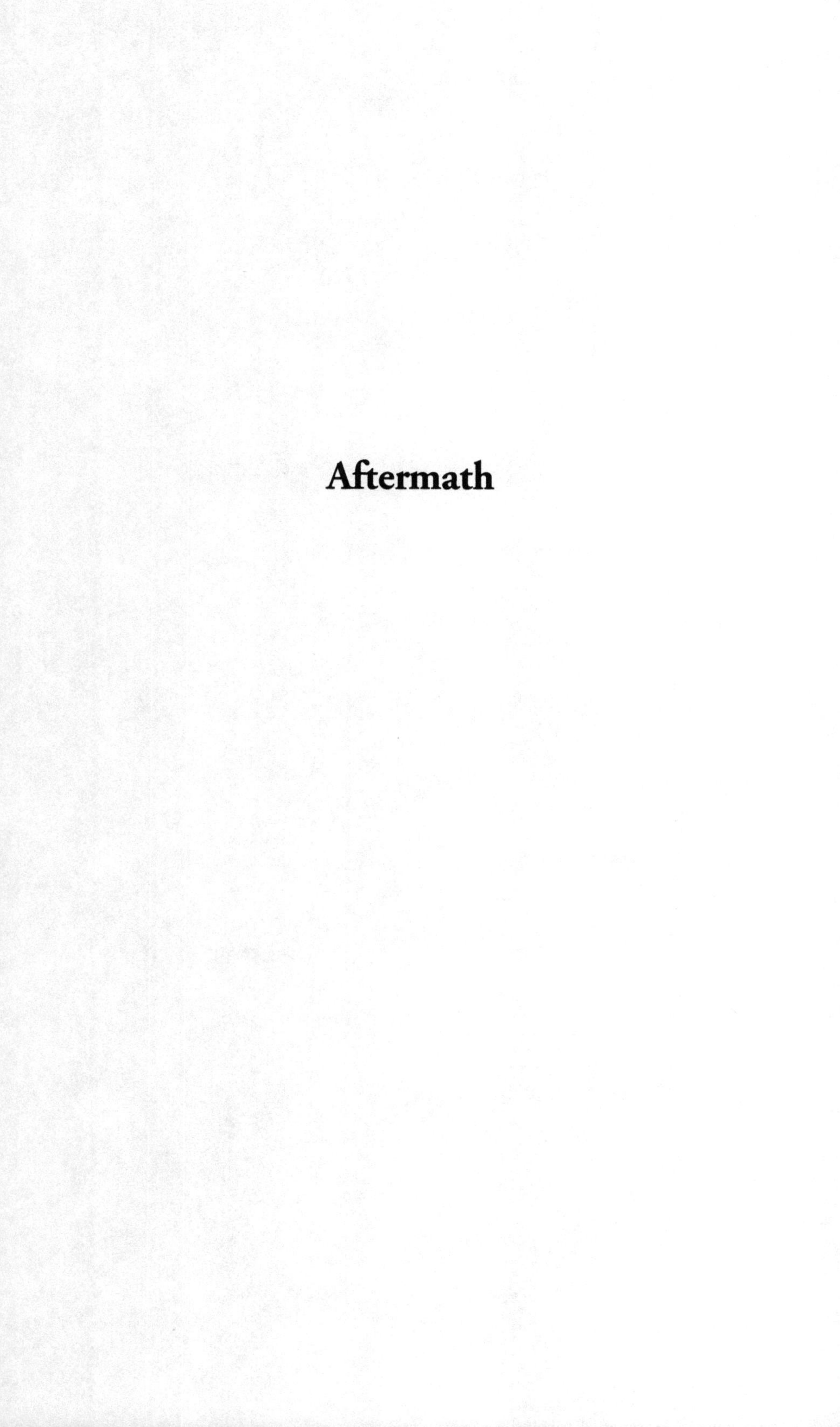

Aftermath

Every Breath You Take

July 18, 1983. Five years later.

Woohoo! It's the eighties!

It had been five years since I had gotten out of jail. I had suffered a few bumps and bruises along the way, but what worthy twenty-something soul hasn't?

I did go home to my parents' house. I lived there for a year, working for my dad in his San Francisco shoe store. One day I came into my parents' kitchen before work, dressed in my best shoe salesman's suit and tie. My mom was at the kitchen table interviewing a guy to be her assistant with around-the-house stuff. He was a very gregarious fellow. Quite a character.

I said hello, took a sip of orange juice, and, while looking over the glass more closely, said, "I think I know you from somewhere."

He blushed and said flirtatiously, "I'll bet you do, honey!"

With that, my mom must've thought, *Oh boy. Out of jail and coming out too!* But that wasn't it. (Not that there's anything wrong with that.)

On my BART commute over to the city, it dawned on me in the tunnel under the Bay. That was Reggie, our cellblock secretary! What were the odds? Then I thought, *I'd better call my dad and tell him that hiring this guy may not be the best plan. I mean, we should at least find out why he was most recently housed in Vacaville State Prison.* So my dad called his best buddy Judge Golde (who still carried a torch for my mother) and accessed the guy's rap sheet. This was totally illegal to do, by the way.

Stan found out he had been in prison for "mayhem." That was the official charge. The actual crime was that during an encounter with a trick, he had bitten off the client's penis. Needless to say, Mommy did not hire him. Honestly, the more shocking part of this story was that she'd considered hiring him at all—why would my mother need an assistant when her week consisted mostly of playing tennis five days a week?

I hated not helping Reggie, as he had been so kind to me, and I know we violated laws in searching his past. I know Reggie had so many less opportunities than I had. I guess I just wanted nothing to do with that part of my past.

One thing I also hated was selling shoes, but I saved every penny so I could move down to San Diego, reunite with Amber, and go back to school. After my eventual move, it became quite evident that Amber's interests were now focused elsewhere. Oh, I tried, but to her credit, she realized that we were not a good fit. Thank God. They always said she was the gang leader.

We had a few fits and starts, but mostly fits. We did have a great summer, though, when Brooke moved there and lived with me and four other girls. I lived in a greenhouse in our backyard. We went to the beach every day, watched *General Hospital* every afternoon (Luke and Laura, baby!), and partied every night.

After flunking out of San Diego State (hey, you try it!), I moved to Los Angeles and attempted to pursue the only thing I really ever wanted to do: write for television. I knew nothing and nobody, which was getting me absolutely nowhere, but I found a place in the Beverly Glen canyon (on the bottom floor of David Hasselhoff's fiancée's place) and played the well-versed role of struggling L.A. writer. With some help from my dad (yes, again), I got a job as a traveling shoe salesman, which I was also terrible at, to pay the rent.

But at the same time, I was also sharing a house in Oakland with my best buddy, Jim, who played piano in our local bar. Now I had two places—and lo and behold, this bar became my third home away from these other two homes. The Oakland bar was like my *Cheers*, a show I had become obsessed with. The brilliant writing and directing and incredible acting were seemingly always seamless. I stayed home every Thursday night with absolute devotion to carefully watch and dissect every line (always alone, in order to better absorb things). Fortunately, this obsession did not make me miss the arrival of the person who was to become my exact girl (my Diane?) one night at the bar: Carole. She was smart and educated and beautiful and talented and fun and funny. I was dumb and lucky.

I had been a bar patron for two years, dropping by almost every night when in town, waiting for this girl. Carole gave me her number and told me "not to call." I called her the next morning. (And she complains that I don't listen to her now.) Two weeks later—after calling her every day—I caught her in a weak moment (apparently after a shopping spree), and she agreed to go out with me. Of course, I took Walker along for approval.

This date has lasted almost forty years . . . and counting. I did have to drag her back from Europe, where she was studying to become an interpreter at the United Nations. I moved her back with me caveman-style, albeit into Diana Ross's former mansion in Beverly Hills (my boss's place), where we lived while it was being renovated.

Every step I took with Carole would turn out well. I had written a *Cheers* sample script and was able to sneak onto the Paramount lot where the show was filmed—it was a lot easier then than it is now. I made my way to the writers'/creators' offices and found a lonely secretary. This was where this vaunted production emanated from? *Cheers* was on "hiatus" between seasons two and three; in Hollywood, this means an unpaid break between seasons to allow all the creative juices to replenish themselves. I schmoozed the very bored secretary, and she agreed to read my script. Mere hours later I got a call. *Hollywood, here I am!*

"Yeah, your script is okay, but it's a far cry from what our writers are able to do."

Well, duh. They had only assembled the greatest comedy writers in the history of television. What had I possibly been thinking? And this assessment was from a bored secretary.

I answered, "Look, I'll do anything to be around there. I'll pour coffee. I'll fetch lunches. I'll refill that Sparkletts bottle [I had no idea how that was done] that is behind you. Anything."

This was my big chance. I was twenty-seven years old, a little long in the tooth to be doing this—almost too late. Luckily, I looked young and was immature, so I passed for twenty-two. She must've taken mercy on me, or pity. Either way, she agreed to have me meet the PA who hired other PAs. "PA" stands for "production assistant," a traditionally horrible job with little benefits and no money—but after twelve interviews, and at the agreed-upon salary of $75 a week, it was mine!

By the grace of God, within a day I was shifted to director Jimmy Burrows's personal assistant, which lowered my work hours from up to fourteen a day to no more than four. Plus, now they were spent hanging out on the *Cheers* stage!

That stage was like a bar, a perpetually fun and funny one. I had found Norm and Nirvana. I loved everything about my job and my life with the love of my life. I could go on forever about the magical moments, but let's just say they were plentiful. *Cheers* was my new family. We had parties and celebrations and births (Emma is one of over fifty *Cheers* babies born during the eleven-year run) and joy. I've got lifelong friends from that place. I could not believe my luck . . . all because of that one larcenous expedition onto the Paramount lot. I've now been involved in over six hundred episodes of television.

Where Everybody Knows Your Name

July 18, 1993. Five great years later.

Carole and I had been married for almost five years. She had become a legendary music teacher in Hollywood—she's nothing if not multi-talented and resourceful. We had an incredible baby girl,

Emma, and another one, Lily, on the way. We were living the dream in the Hollywood Hills. *Cheers* had just ended; thanks to everyone's incredible generosity, I had been able to direct a couple of episodes, and (poorly) write another. This was just fifteen years after my release from prison. I was about to work on *Frasier*, directing episodes there and on other shows.

Take Me Out to the Ball Game

April 21, 2010. Thirty-Two Years After Jail.

In 2010, I went to San Diego to go to a San Francisco Giants game with Brooke, Amber, and Amber's husband, the latter a local sports celebrity. While he was busy schmoozing with a bunch of jock-sniffers, I was sitting there next to Amber, losing two hundred bucks watching my team lose to the fucking Padres. (What a stupid name for a team, anyway.) I remember this year because it was the season we miraculously won our first World Championship in my lifetime.

While watching the meaningless early-season game, Amber casually turned to me and said, "You know, I was selling drugs out of the Sports Page before I ever met you."

The umpire called the next pitch outside, and future Hall of Famer, then rookie "Buster" Posey threw the ball back to the pitcher. A moment later, her words sank in. We had never talked about our times in jail. I really did not know this girl.

Slowly turning to her, I managed, "What?"

With a sheepish kind of smile, she said, "Yeah."

I know. Scintillating conversation going on here.

I replied, "You mean, I've felt guilty about all this, especially about dragging you into it, and now you tell me you actually were selling drugs before me?"

Jesus. Maybe Gustine had been right. I am dumb.

I turned back to the game, and even though the Giants lost, I felt a whole hell of a lot better. A lot of guilt left my soul that day. I should've been angry, but I wasn't—just very glad things turned out the way they did. It ended that chapter for me in a very satisfying way. I was supposed to stay overnight, but I scooted back up to L.A. and into the comfort of my family.

Don't You Worry 'Bout a Thing

July 18, 2018. Forty years later.

I am writing this because my daughter Lily found a letter I had written to Judge Golde from prison. It was written on that day when he and my dad came to visit me in Vacaville.

I had been waiting for one of my girls to hit rock bottom before I told them the story of *my* lowest period, and how lowest moments do not necessarily have to define you. That it's not the end. But that moment never came. Lucky—because when Lily found the letter and I got home to explain I had been in jail, she burst into hysterical laughter. Then she fielded a phone call from her boyfriend and went into her bedroom.

Carole and I were perplexed. When we followed her into her room, she held her hand over the receiver and gently whispered up to me, "I don't give a fuck."

Carole said, "Lil, Dad was in prison for five months, you know."

Lily's eyes popped. She hung up the phone. "*What?* Does Emma know?"

No, we said, she didn't, which prompted an immediate cross-country phone call to her sister. After Lily asked Emma if she had known that "Dad had been in prison" and got the requisite "no," she explained it had been for five months. From across the country through the phone came gales of laughter. Glad I didn't waste my best fastball on these two.

Then she hung up with Emma and told me I should write a book about this (which is something I had been mulling over for forty years). She said to tailor it to give encouragement to millennials, who are struggling with lost faith and despair. So, since it happened exactly forty years before I started writing, I guess it's all worked out perfectly.

There is so much that is able to be accomplished. It doesn't matter how low you've gotten.

As I say to every kid I talk to who wants to get into the television industry, "Hey, if I can do it, anyone can."

It's just a bunch of human beings doing these jobs. All it takes is a combination of talent, timing, and luck. I've had a lot of luck.

The End

June 18, 2023. Present Day.

Wait! Not so fast.

I called Lorimar. He doesn't remember the case. That's fair. He'd tossed it off to Kunkle right away. Kunkle was Lorimar's best friend, and I don't want to trash him; he died in 2000.

I reached out to Gustine. He claims he doesn't remember the case, but I don't believe him. Either the sharpest legal minds do not end up practicing in Butte County, or Gustine is lying. I suspect both. I let him off. Who cares? I won.

I'm bringing this book to my dad for Father's Day. He doesn't know I wrote it. He won't like revisiting it, but I want to thank him for everything he did (and has done) for me. He was there with constant love and support (mentally, emotionally, and financially); it couldn't have been easy, and I couldn't have gotten through the experience nearly as well as I did without him. He's ninety-five and going strong. My mom passed away in 2018. After prison, she and I really got close. I miss her.

And I could not live (nor would I want to) without my wife Carole. We've been married thirty-one years, and I can only hope for thirty-one more. Sometimes I think she hopes for less than thirty-one more minutes. I hope she doesn't always feel that way. Honey, I love you so very much. You are my exact type.